Modern Cata

Modern Catalan Plays

edited by

John London and David George

The Quarrelsome Party
by Joan Brossa

The Audition
by Rodolf Sirera

Desire
by Josep Maria Benet i Jornet

Fourplay
by Sergi Belbel

Methuen

Published by Methuen 2000

1 3 5 7 9 10 8 6 4 2

Caution

All rights whatsoever in these plays are strictly reserved and application for
performances etc. should be made to: *The Quarrelsome Party* and *The Audition*: John
London, 14 Leigh Street, London WC1H 9EW; *Desire* and *Fourplay*: Sharon G.
Feldman, Department of Spanish and Portuguese, University of Kansas, Lawrence,
Kansas 66045, USA. No performance may be given unless a licence has been
obtained.

Contents

The publication of this book was made possible by a grant from the Institució de les Lletres Catalanes in Barcelona. The anthology is dedicated to the memory of Joan Brossa (1919–1998), the poet and father of Catalan avant-garde theatre, who died as the volume was being completed.

Acknowledgements

The editors are grateful to the playwrights included in this anthology for their assistance with the translators' queries. They would also like to thank the following for their advice: Maria Antònia Babí i Vila, Maria Delgado, Rosanna Eadie, Hans-Peter Kellner, Pepa Llopis, Andreu Rossinyol, Dídac Teixidor and Alan Yates. Some of John London's work was financed by the Alexander von Humboldt-Stiftung and the Leverhulme Trust. Michael Earley of Methuen supported this project through all its stages.

INTRODUCTION

If a major publisher had produced an anthology of Catalan plays twenty or even fifteen years ago, the introduction to such a collection would inevitably have sounded apologetic. Any argument for attention would have contained sentences full of worthy excuses: 'Hardly anybody outside Spain, or in some cases, hardly anybody outside Catalonia, has heard of these playwrights, but they have nonetheless written some exciting drama.' 'The minority status of this Romance language should not obscure the quality of its theatre.'

Now, at the beginning of a new millennium, there is no need for a defensive tone. Following the 1992 Olympic Games, Barcelona acquired a confident, new international status as the capital of Catalonia. The relaxation of anti-Catalan censorship after the death of General Franco in 1975 and a degree of regional autonomy have led to a flourishing cultural life. There is a vibrant literature in Catalan, continuing a tradition going back to the Middle Ages. Although memories may remain of the public burning of Catalan books at the beginning of the dictatorship (in 1939), the long, dark period of Francoism is at an end. Catalan is now taught in schools and universities. Catalan radio exists alongside Catalan television. There are daily newspapers in Catalan. Catalan translations of foreign books sometimes appear before Spanish translations.

This new assertiveness has meant that the traffic is not all one-way and that Joan Miró and Salvador Dalí are not the only Catalans famous abroad. Ventura Pons has gained a cult following for his films, like *Caresses*, shot entirely with Catalan dialogue. Having been a linchpin of theatre in Barcelona, Lluís Pasqual went on to become director of the Spanish National Theatre in Madrid (1983–1989) and artistic director of the Théâtre de l'Europe at the Odéon in Paris in the 1990s. Anyone attending international theatre festivals will be familiar with the eye-catching antics of Catalan performance groups such as Els Joglars, La Cubana, La Fura dels Baus and Comediants. (The last two staged the opening and closing ceremonies to the Barcelona Olympic Games.)

Without the fireworks and mass spectacles of such companies, a few Catalan playwrights have already established a considerable reputation. Lluïsa Cunillé's *The Meeting* was commissioned as part of the Edinburgh International Festival in 1999. Josep Maria Benet i Jornet's play in this volume, *Desire*, has been translated into Spanish, French and German. Rodolf Sirera's *The Audition* has had Spanish, English, Italian, Portuguese, Greek and French productions. Sergi Belbel, the youngest and most performed writer in this selection, has been applauded throughout Europe. His play *After the Rain* was produced Off-Broadway in New York and both the Royal Court and the Gate theatres in London have presented his work. Joan Brossa's highly original visual art is regularly exhibited in non-Spanish galleries. When it was first displayed in Great Britain, in 1992, the London listings magazine *Time Out* called the exhibition 'a brilliant, unmissable show'.

The inroads made by these dramatists are not merely spontaneous instances of international recognition. They reflect an increased theatrical infrastructure in Catalonia and the Valencia region. This practical and financial backing accompanied the renewed enthusiasm of directors for contemporary plays during the late 1980s, in opposition to collective creation and the visually impressive, but largely non-verbal, productions of more famous performance groups. Although the composition of the plays in this anthology spans three decades, it was a significant acknowledgement of a developing tradition of dramatic writing that all four of them were given revivals or premieres in Barcelona during 1990-1993.

Some thirty auditoria of differing sizes testify to Barcelona's theatrical vitality. In 1997, the impressive multi-space National Theatre of Catalonia opened in the city. The distribution of the seven million people who speak Catalan extends well beyond Catalonia. Valencia, the Balearic Islands, Roussillon (in France), Alghero (in Sardinia) and Andorra all have Catalan-speaking inhabitants. Yet, in the realm of theatre, as with so many other cultural manifestations, Barcelona is proving itself to be the leading force.

For at least the last twenty years of his life, Joan Brossa (1919–1998) had become a legendary figure in the Catalan capital. Few in the world of Catalan art and literature were unaware of this ironic, shabby little man, who went to see one film a day and never seemed to fit into any movement, fashion or period. Taxi-drivers would talk about photographs they had seen of his apparently chaotic studio where piles of newspapers carpeted the floor.

Such images are misleading. Brossa's sloppy exterior concealed a razor-sharp wit and he was always ready with an aphorism or relevant insight to comment on an important event. His art works, or 'object poems' as he called them, had won him many admirers after being seen in huge exhibitions. Brossa drew on Marcel Duchamp's aesthetic of the 'found object' to juxtapose sometimes commonplace materials, highlighting a previously unperceived beauty in these things and revealing contradictory or self-defeating ideas. A pencil has a pool of ink which appears to be leaking from it. Dice are round and can therefore never land on any single number. A mask hides the complete identity of playing cards.

If these works have a certain theatricality, Brossa considered all his artistic output as poetry. His written verse was initially influenced by surrealism, but he later experimented with classical forms and also evolved a unique style to describe seemingly banal activities. Some of his poems consist merely in the recording of actions, the neutral depiction of interiors and the transcription of fragments of dialogue. They often resemble the instructions in Brossa's short theatrical pieces, or happenings (well before the term had been coined). From this perspective it is easier to understand why Brossa stated that he began to write for the theatre from 'an internal need to find the fourth dimension of the poem'. His range was enormous and the man who once claimed that art only interested him 'as an adventure' wrote over three hundred titles as examples of his theatrical explorations.

Within this diversity *The Quarrelsome Party* (1963) possesses
many features that locate it firmly in the period in which it
was written. The first act reveals the effects on a working-class
family of Barcelona's great snowfall of 1962. By the end of the
second act, a group of upper-class old people are lamenting
the death of Enric Borràs (which actually occurred in 1957
when the actor was ninety-four). Their dialogue is cluttered
with the roles he played in well-known Catalan and Spanish
plays: *Marta of the Lowlands* by Àngel Guimerà (1845–1924),
The Great Galeoto, by José Echegaray (1832–1916), *The Mayor
of Zalamea*, by Pedro Calderón de la Barca (1600–1681) and
The Old Folks, by Ignasi Iglésias (1871–1928).

These details form just part of a larger picture in which a
realistic style mixes with the sort of quirky, sometimes
incoherent, dialogue to be found in the theatre of the absurd.
The success of *The Quarrelsome Party* in 1992 was founded not
on nostalgia, but on consummate dramatic skill. The
inexplicable entrances and exits in the second act parody the
ridiculous conventions of the *sainet*, or one-act popular
comedy. All the characters speak a language which is
teasingly difficult to translate, because it often sounds
proverbial, but is in fact a poetic invention of Brossa himself:
'I might be breathless, but I know I'm on the right track';
'Wherever anybody sits down to eat, the tablecloth ends up
dirty.' Such phrases anticipate the imagination of the shop
assistant in the third act, who describes an ancient Greek past
with the help of feature films. Throughout the play there are
pointed criticisms of those with power and contrasts quickly
emerge between the rich and the poor, the creatively dreamy
and the cynically materialistic. In a way common to all
Brossa's art, what he called his 'theatrical poetry' derives its
impact as much from the juxtaposition of elements as from
their intrinsic meaning.

Although *The Audition* (1978) is dedicated to Brossa, Rodolf
Sirera (b. 1948) has always maintained a much more practical
involvement in theatrical productions than his older
colleague. He played an important role in creating anti-
Francoist protest performances in the Valencia region and,

with the onset of democracy, subsequently worked in government to develop Valencian theatre. Both on his own and in collaboration with his brother Josep Lluís Sirera (b. 1954) he has written a considerable body of plays in the Valencian dialect of Catalan, including political satires, historical dramas, experimental texts and social comedies.

Whereas, towards the end of Francoism, Sirera declared that theatre was 'a political weapon', *The Audition* at first sight seems distant from such a committed stance. Having served his guest with a mysterious drink, the Marquis wants the actor Gabriel to perform Socrates's death scene and it looks as though the theatrical equivalent of a snuff movie is about to be re-enacted. The Marquis's tricksy manipulation of the antidote adds to the suspense. But this is not simply an eighteenth-century variation on Anthony Shaffer's *Sleuth*. The Catalan title of the play means 'the poison or drug of theatre' and that, bolstered by the mention of Socrates, gives much of the plot away from the start.

What Sirera adds to this context is a debate stemming from *Paradoxe sur le comédien* by Denis Diderot, who died in 1784, the same year in which *The Audition* is set. Diderot was keen to differentiate between actors who drew on genuine feeling and those who were more premeditated and self-controlled. In the course of Sirera's play the Marquis is, in some respects, the more successful actor, even though he is not a professional. Meanwhile, Gabriel's fear destroys in minutes all his career has taught him. (Socrates's life, free from artifice, is a suitable vehicle for removing technique.) But the Marquis is in search of a natural performance and, by promoting reality and killing his guest, also puts an end to theatre. Gabriel's acting for real obviously has to take place once the final blackout has occurred.

The Marquis has a philosophical as well as an aesthetic justification for his behaviour. Behind his reasoning lies the sophist Antiphon's idea that laws are sovereign in front of witnesses, but in their absence, man resorts to the laws of nature. We have made laws for the eyes. (Unlike accounts by Plato, the text by Xenophon, upon which the Marquis's play is supposedly based, does not mention Socrates's faith in an afterlife.) The cruelty resulting from such arguments on the eve of the French Revolution can but evoke the actions of the Marquis de Sade. By annihilating the falsity of theatre, Sirera's Marquis is, despite his social superiority, very much the revolutionary. Three years after the death of Franco, the play raises different questions. The Marquis may behave like a dictator, but his quest for authenticity constitutes an attack on the artificiality of a whole approach to theatre and life. In the transition to democracy, is it better to judge and condemn all the protagonists of the old regime? Or should we let their lies and fictional view of the past go unchallenged in favour of the maintenance of a new political construction which, in its own way, is perhaps just as artificial?

Ever since the premiere of his first play, *An Old, Familiar Smell*, in 1964, Josep Maria Benet i Jornet (b. 1940) has been celebrated for his direct and allegorical portrayals of the socio-political reality of Spain. Like Sirera, he was influenced by Brecht and repeatedly pursued the symbolic value of stories and myths. Yet there are also more personal components in his plays which have gradually become more prominent as time has elapsed since the end of Francoism. Benet is probably best known to British audiences through *Actresses* (1996) and *Beloved/Friend* (1998), Ventura Pons's film versions of two of his recent dramas.

Desire (1989) is the development of a form initially sketched in Benet's own dialogue of 1977, *The Beechwood*. Both texts are indebted to the style of Harold Pinter's three short pieces *Landscape*, *Silence* and *Night*, while the spotlit faces in *Desire* recall a similar technique in Beckett's *Not I*. Within these echoes, Benet constructs his own mystery, as his four unnamed characters, two men and two women, meet, argue, move apart and express themselves in staccato dialogues and poetic monologues. The settings – a country house, a road and a cafeteria – are as undefined as the characters' intentions. We never quite know if allusions or events are sinister or banal. Dialogue conceals as much as it reveals. Are the anonymous phone calls a real threat? Does the tension between husband and wife hide a deeper conflict in the past?

Does she perhaps know the other man and woman? Are their meetings planned or accidental?

Faced by the constant presence of these questions, it is not surprising that reviewers have mentioned Alfred Hitchcock in connection with the menacing atmosphere in *Desire*. The ambiguous sexuality in the play, together with the importance of the husband's chisel, provoke comparisons with Paul Verhoeven's film *Basic Instinct*, released three years after Benet's drama. In fact, the chisel is a homage to Guimerà's Catalan play of 1897, *Marta of the Lowlands*, in which a knife has an equivalent relevance. Besides, it would be wrong to limit the impact of *Desire* to the ostensible reconciliation of the two women in what could be an acknowledgement of their shared past. These final moments do not clarify everything which has preceded them. Emotional fear and the threat of memory have in the meantime created different levels of reality, so that previous encounters may well have been imagined rather than real. The full significance of *Desire* lies as much in the value attached to these scenes as in a simple explanation for them. Benet once said that he liked to think of a play as a beautiful building, in which one part depends on the other.

Benet was in close contact with his friend Sergi Belbel (b. 1963) during the genesis of *Desire* and Belbel eventually directed its premiere production in Barcelona. The collaboration between these two dramatists forms a direct bridge between two distinct generations. While playwrights such as Sirera, Benet and Jordi Teixidor produced their first drama as a reaction to the Francoist dictatorship in which they were living, Belbel, and young writers like Lluïsa Cunillé, Jordi Galceran and Jordi Sànchez, have felt relatively liberated from the shadow of Francoism and the need either to conform or rebel.

Belbel has been at the forefront of this younger generation of dramatists through the success of his plays (in Spain and abroad) and his wider theatrical activity in Catalonia. As well as bringing the lesser-known works of Beckett and Pinter to wider attention, he has translated Bernard-Marie Koltès into

Catalan and directed his own translations of texts by Heiner
Müller and Georges Perec. Belbel's plays are constantly
innovative. He has experimented with ingenious plot
structures, monologues and the total immobility of actors. His
dialogue contains enormous sentences with apparently
nonsensical, repeated words and an erratic form of
punctuation. Some of these idiosyncrasies have consequences
for intonation: a question without a question mark does not
have the same pronounced interrogative tone as if the
question mark were present. Other peculiarities should affect
actors in different ways: parentheses within a speech can
indicate a switch of tone; an exclamation mark followed by a
comma can convey a continued, almost breathless delivery.
With their tendency to lapse into generalisations and poetic
contemplations, their lack of immediately clear motives and
their frequent inability to be totally serious, Belbel's
characters have much in common with the strange world of
Hal Hartley's films.

Fourplay (1989) is a good example of Belbel's style, at once
simple and convoluted. The Catalan title means the nuptial
or marriage bed (which dominates the stage) and the premise
of the farcical plot is as straightforward as its setting: one
couple tries to make another couple meet and sleep together
in this new item of furniture. But the thirty-eight scenes are
not a logical progression. The odd-numbered scenes take the
action forward, while the even-numbered scenes go back in
time. We therefore see the final moment right after the
beginning, although things are complicated further by the
repetition of all scenes in a differing guise. (The centre of the
play is a kind of mirror in scenes nineteen and twenty.)

The result of these formal games is not merely a
satisfaction in gradually appreciating the symmetry of a
baroque structure. The truncated nature of all the scenes
when they are first played means that we initially understand
only part of what is going on. When they are performed in a
more complete version our perception changes and sometimes contradicts earlier views. The female friend seems
extrovert and sexy in the first half, but in the second she is a
poor, pathetic secretary desperate to be somebody she is not.

(The second time round, her striptease is not erotic.) Nerves and a series of misunderstandings prevent the bed from actually being used. As members of the audience we make mistaken interpretations just like the characters. Frustration, perplexity and annoyance are the main sources of humour in the play, but they are also the reason for its outcome.

This is the *reductio ad absurdissimum* of bedroom farce. Like the best Catalan dramatists before him, Belbel is reassessing a tradition in order to give it fresh life.

John London, September 1999

Further Reading

Belbel, Sergi, *Deep Down*, trans. by John London, *Modern International Drama*, 26, no. 2 (Spring 1993), 5–24.

    After the Rain, trans. by David George, John London and Xavier Rodríguez Rosell, in Klaus Chatten, *Sugar Dollies*/Sergi Belbel, *After the Rain* (London: Methuen, 1996).

    Caresses, trans. by John London, in *Spanish Plays*, ed. by Elyse Dodgson and Mary Peate (London: Nick Hern Books, 1999).

    Blood, trans. by Marion Peter Holt, unpublished.

Benet i Jornet, Josep Maria, *The Ship*, trans. by George E. Wellwarth, in *3 Catalan Dramatists*, ed. by George E. Wellwarth (Montreal: Engendra Press, 1976).

    Legacy, trans. by Eulàlia Borràs and Janet de Cesaris, Estreno Contemporary Spanish Plays, 17 (Delaware, OH: Estreno, 2000).

    Stages, trans. by Marion Peter Holt, unpublished.

    Fleeting, trans. by Marion Peter Holt, unpublished.

Brossa, Joan, 'Ten Accio-Spectacles' [*sic*], trans. by Alain Arias-Misson, *Chicago Review*, 18, nos. 3–4 (1966), 78–82.

Catalan Writing, no. 16 (June 1999). Special issue on Catalan theatre, with all articles in English.

Cunillé, Lluïsa, *The Meeting*, trans. by John London, in Lluïsa Cunillé, *The Meeting*/David Greig, *The Speculator* (London: Methuen, 1999).

Delgado, Maria, and David George, 'Sergi Belbel', in *Modern Spanish Dramatists: A Bio-Bibliographical Sourcebook*, ed. by Mary Parker (Westport, CT: Greenwood Press, 2000).

Estreno, 24, no. 2 (Autumn 1998). Special issue (devoted to Catalan theatre) of a North-American periodical, with articles in English, Spanish and Catalan.

Feldman, Sharon G., '"Un agujero sin límites": la mirada fenomenológica de Josep M. Benet i Jornet', *Anales de la Literatura Española Contemporánea*, 24 (1999).

George, David, and John London, eds, *Contemporary Catalan Theatre: An Introduction* (Sheffield: Anglo-Catalan Society, 1996).

Gilabert i Barberà, Pau, 'The Tradition of the Death of Socrates as a Good Paradigm of the "Poison of Drama": Reflections on Rodolf Sirera's *El verí del teatre / The Poison of Drama*', *International Journal of the Classical Tradition* (forthcoming).

Guimerà, Àngel, *Marta of the Lowlands*, trans. by Wallace Gillpatrick (Garden City, NY: Doubleday, 1914).

Joan Brossa o les paraules són les coses (Barcelona: Fundació Joan Miró, 1986). Exhibition catalogue with essays translated into English.

Joan Brossa: Words are Things: Poems, Objects and Installations (London: Riverside Studios, 1992). Exhibition catalogue with essays in English and translations of texts by Brossa.

Ragué-Arias, María-José, *El teatro de fin de milenio en España: (De 1975 hasta hoy)* (Barcelona: Ariel, 1996).

Wellwarth, George E., ed., *3 Catalan Dramatists* (Montreal: Engendra Press, 1976).

The Quarrelsome Party
A Play in Three Acts

by

Joan Brossa

translated by

**Anna García Jové, Laia Castañé,
David George and John London**

Premiere in Catalan

Teatre Poliorama, Barcelona, 24 July 1992, directed by
Hermann Bonnín.

Characters

Act One
Old Woman
Daughter
Old Man
Son

Act Two
First Old Woman
Second Old Woman
First Old Man

Act Three
Old Woman
Daughter
Old Man
The Shop Assistant
A Customer

Act One

Dark background. On stage, the **Old Woman**. *She is rubbing her hands together because of the cold.*

Daughter (*enters*)   What a blizzard! My God!

Old Woman   Now the snow will be the perfect excuse for everything.

Daughter   Mrs Neptunia, have you ever seen such a bad one?

Old Woman   No, no. Although my character has been tested many a time. When I dig my heels in, it's because I'm right.

Daughter   The street is deserted; it looks as if life has come to a standstill.

Old Woman   Do you think the trams are running?

Daughter   Of course not! It's so quiet! Only the sound of the snow falling. Everything is so white!

Old Woman   It must be a sorry sight! I don't want to go out.

Daughter   All the cars have stopped and they're covered in a blanket of snow.

Old Woman   And how will we manage if the dustmen don't come?

Daughter   Why should they come if everything has stopped?

Old Woman   What will become of us?

Daughter   We have to keep calm, Mrs Neptunia. On the radio they said that essential supplies won't be affected.

Old Woman   Personally, I don't like the situation at all. Didn't you just say everything had stopped?

Daughter   Yes, but . . . (*The lights go out.*) Oh!

Old Woman   What? Did they mention that on the radio? Oh, gosh! Well if that makes them happy.

Daughter   I haven't done the books.

Old Woman   How are we going to get to market? Tell me.

Daughter   If it hadn't snowed so much . . .

Old Woman   But the fact is it has. There's no bread in the bakery. It's all pain and suffering. And what are we supposed to do with two days' worth of rubbish?

Daughter   We've been told to burn it.

Old Woman   Nothing is working, girl. It's us, the old people, who suffer the most. What are we going to do if we run out of coal, now that there's no oil? Money is the main problem. Don't you think it's a crime that there's no oil?

Daughter   I don't agree. All my dresses have been patched up again and again.

Old Woman   Anything can make us lose our temper. It's so sad! My husband was a tax officer for the town and I don't think anybody has ever matched him. Although while he was alive, I thought he was worthless. And he thought the same about me. While we were married, we always said no to everything. And, as you can see, in the end, it was yes, because he was the first to die.

Daughter   How old was Johnny when your husband died?

Old Woman   Thirteen. OK, go and fetch a candle, would you? Eh, girl?

Daughter   My father told me he's coming down straight away.

Old Woman   Are you the only ones in the flat?

Daughter   Yes, we are. And, believe me, it's colder than it is here. The terrace roof is just by us . . .

Old Woman   But you've got a very nice view from the balcony.

Daughter   Yes, it's very high up.

Old Woman   And you said he was coming down now? He's a naughty devil!

Daughter   It's as though we were living in a town in Scandinavia.

Old Woman   Your father is a devil!

Daughter   I don't know, I've never thought he was like that.

Old Woman   Many things draw your father and me together, and they create a rift between us.

Daughter   Why?

Old Woman   When we were young, people were never fair about us. Your mother was as stubborn as a mule. She couldn't stand your father's character. And yet, she was a very good friend of my husband. But I don't know why I'm telling you all of this. Believe me, I'm very pleased to be on good terms with your father again.

Daughter   He's not unhappy about it either.

Old Woman   How do you know?

Daughter   Sometimes, daddy seems to be thinking out loud, and I'm the kind of person who picks things up easily.

Old Woman   Your mother made everything so complicated . . . (*The lights come on.*) About time!

Daughter   Great! People's characters change so much!

Old Woman   In a play, do you prefer the plot or the characters?

Daughter   I don't know: if it's necessary, I can always change my behaviour.

Old Woman   I like complicated plots, even if the characters don't develop very much, do you know what I mean? What I really like is that everybody gets their just deserts in the end. Otherwise, why should we stay in this world for such a long time? Each of us has already built up hopes about what we should receive in the next life, although sometimes we won't admit it. (*She points to her heart.*) That's where we have our hopes. You've turned out like your father.

Daughter   And Johnny?

Old Woman   My son is all heart, just like my husband.

Daughter   Really?

Old Man (*enters*)   Hello, Neptunia! What a snowfall, eh! Have the lights gone out here as well? Why do the authorities allow such things to happen? And what about the people who live here and have to manage in all this snow? If *we* don't clear the snow from the streets, nobody else'll do it. Politicians are useless! They're only interested in money! And this affects us all.

Old Woman   Has somebody slammed the door in your face?

Old Man   They can die for all I care. They're just hopeless politicians: they're only good at giving orders; believe me.

Old Woman   Is that what you think, Tony?

Old Man   Where's your son ?

Old Woman   He's just gone to clear the snow from our neighbours' balcony. You know, the ones who live on the third floor.

Daughter   At Sinetti's? She never welcomes a helping hand.

Old Woman   It was her husband who came. He didn't want him to bother us, so he went straight up to clear the snow.

Daughter   He'll get soaked, poor man!

Old Man   Forget it, let's get back to where I was.

Old Woman   Shall I tell you what I'm interested in?

Old Man   You're not up to it.

Old Woman   Me? Is that what you think?

Old Man   I'll prove you wrong, just as you've been many times before.

Old Woman   And you come here to speak about humanity? You?

Old Man (*to his* **Daughter**)   Lola: didn't I tell you on Thursday it would snow?

Daughter   Yes, father.

Old Man   And what did the met office say?

Daughter   They said the weather would stay fine over the whole country and it would get even milder.

Old Man   There you are, that's the way things go!

Old Woman   I know, they never get things right!

Old Man (*to his* **Daughter**)   Lola: what's the riddle I told you about, you know, the one you couldn't solve?

Daughter   One and two and three and four, half of twenty-four; twenty-four and twenty-five, two and three and four and twenty.

Old Man   That's it. (*The lights go out.*)

Old Woman   Oh dear!

Old Man   Damn!

Daughter   Oh!

Old Man   Are you convinced now that I'm not just being stubborn? (*He takes a candlestick and a candle out of his pocket and lights the candle.*) If it weren't for me!

Old Woman   Forget it: only a real disaster could have caused so many problems.

Old Man   Have you got any bread left, Neptunia?

Old Woman   A loaf of bread and a loaf of bread and a half: how much does that make?

Old Man   Two loaves and a half, isn't it?

Old Woman   Right!

Daughter   This morning I saw people skiing in the streets.

Old Man   And they certainly couldn't ski very well, poor things!

Old Woman   We'll see how this all ends.

Daughter   And I also saw some people dressed in ski suits, without any skis.

Old Man   They were showing off. I hope the gods protect us from this evil.

Old Woman   A lot of people must be falling over in the streets at the moment!

Daughter   It's a terrible pity the snow causes so many problems. The streets look so nice covered in white!

Old Man   There isn't any kind of help: the council services are nowhere to be seen. In fact, everybody has taken the day off. Believe me!

Old Woman   All extremes are dangerous.

Old Man   I'm not preaching any morality.

Old Woman   I'm always on the lenient side.

Daughter   Nobody expected anything like this.

Old Man   Why? It should be compulsory for official cars or public transport to have tyre chains as well as the usual accessories. It's as old as the hills.

Old Woman   People could fall and break a leg.

Daughter   And Johnny could sprain his arm.

Old Man   We are free citizens, but we're so gullible!

Old Woman   Don't you now consider yourself to be superior?

Old Man   I can't brag any more.

Daughter   That wouldn't surprise me.

Old Man (*to his* **Daughter**)   See, do you still like the snow?

Old Woman   It's a real change, isn't it?

Daughter   Yes, Mrs Neptunia. (*The lights come back on.*) Oh!

Old Man   Huh, about time. (*He puts the candle out.*)

Old Woman   Who's trying to steal the electricity? We've been in the dark for such a long time! Do you think there can be a justifiable reason for this? And what are we going to do if the dustmen don't come?

Son (*enters. His clothes are all covered in snow*)   I think it'll snow again. The cars are still stuck and you can hardly get out of the house. Haven't you heard the fire engine?

Old Woman   Has there been an accident?

Son   The weather has turned against us.

Old Man   Just the weather?

Daughter (*to the* **Son**)   Why don't you change your clothes?

Old Woman   Is anybody blameless?

Son   There's snow hemming us in everywhere.

Old Man   We people melt, I mean, just like snowmen.

Daughter   Come on: why don't you change your clothes?

Old Man   Do you think that will solve our problems?

Son (*to the* **Daughter**)   I can't see that I'm covered in snowflakes or flecks.

Old Woman   I'd like to know if there have been any accidents. We have to be careful not to slip. Remember.

Old Man   You know a lot, Neptunia.

Old Woman (*sighs*)   Well, in my life, I've suffered many injustices in silence. And I can't be accused of having lacked good sense, which is more than you can say for some people. (*To the* **Old Man**.) I've never sought a quarrel with you, and I've never been moved by resentment, although you may not admit it.

Old Man   And me? Have I ever wanted to argue?

Old Woman   Do you think it would have upset me to hear you?

Old Man   I've never needed a doctor. (*To his* **Daughter**.) Tell them that's true, girl.

Daughter   Yes, Father, yes.

Old Woman (*to the* **Old Man**)   Because you're as stubborn as a mule.

Old Man   Me?

Old Woman   Yes, you're the sort of person who likes to have people beg you for things on their knees.

Old Man   And you're the sort who does things behind people's backs.

Old Woman   What are you getting at?

Daughter   Father, don't say unfair things.

Old Man   I'm alive and kicking.

Old Woman   I should know, but you've never fulfilled my wishes. Never!

Old Man   Me?

Daughter   Mrs Neptunia, do you think there's a single blameless person in the world?

Old Woman   The thing is, I've often seen him (*to the* **Old Man**) in front of certain doors.

Old Man   Some time or another you thought I was waiting for you, didn't you? Tell me the truth.

Old Woman   Tony, we'd better not talk about this.

Old Man   I'll tell you more, so that it won't be difficult for you to understand. My wife used to say that the truth about things hardly benefits those who are concerned, if we eventually lessen the burden of their arguments it will reinforce their love.

Old Woman   I've completely missed your point. But certain doors tell tales, you know?

Old Man   I like to make things clear, although it winds me up. I can foresee all the benefits you want so that you can understand my point of view.

Old Woman   I met you long before you met her.

Old Man   Is that her fault?

Old Woman   Don't forget to bear in mind that I make both you and your daughter welcome in my home.

Old Man   Tell me, don't *you* ever bring your son to my home?

Old Woman   And sometimes I stay too long.

Son   Come on: I won't allow you two to go on arguing.

Daughter   I won't either.

Son   Why don't you stop imitating word games?

Old Woman   All right. Provided I don't have to go out.

Old Man   You already know you can always count on our friendship.

Old Woman   I'm still the same.

Old Man   Good girl.

Old Woman   Oh, Tony! Although the years go by, in some ways we don't change and I know the things I'd do.

Old Man   I know, Neptunia. I feel the same way.

Old Woman   Although, sometimes, my age scares me.

Old Man   We'll do all we have to.

Son   Of course, we will, won't we, Lola?

Daughter   I really like it when you come to our home, out of kindness for me and my father.

Old Woman   Men, sometimes, aren't aware of our tears.

Old Man   Neptunia, you don't need to invent excuses.

Old Woman   I'm not avoiding it. You can see I'm speaking about this while they're here.

Old Man   I know a lot about these things. (*Short pause.*) It's getting cold.

Old Woman   To be honest, I can't remember such a heavy snowfall.

Old Man   They've run out of eighty-cent stamps.

Son   I've already told you, we're cut off.

Old Woman   And where are we going to throw all the rubbish? I wish the dustman would come soon. My God!

Son   I think I'll go for a walk.

Old Woman   Where?

Son   On the paths the neighbours have cleared with their shovels. I'll try to go to the main street.

Old Woman   And couldn't the roof cave in because of the snow?

Daughter (*to the* **Son**)   Wait a moment: where are you going now?

Son   I've got some experience with problems caused by snow. When I was at the training camp, it often snowed; but I think this snowfall is heavier than the ones I had to face.

Old Man   The army should help us clear the snow.

Son   *I* know that the few tanks they've got are only used in the passing-out parade on 'Victory Day'. They're out of order for the whole year. And a month before the parade, everybody's in a panic trying to find spare parts.

Old Man   Pss! How do you expect anything to work?

Daughter   It's all just a façade; as we know.

Old Man   Exactly. Once again the facts prove you right.

Son   I've heard our mayor phoned the barracks where Joaquim is doing his military service and, although there are forty soldiers, only fifteen were there. They didn't even know where their colonel was. Usually they all eat out. That way, the officers keep the mess money.

Old Woman   I've never heard anything about that.

Son   Well, *I*'ll be back in a minute.

Daughter   I'd like to go with you.

Old Man   Don't upset me, girl.

Old Woman (*to her* **Son**)   Take care not to slip, Johnny.

Son   Yes, mother. (*He exits.*)

Old Woman   Women must stay inside.

Daughter   As if I didn't have anything better to do.

Old Man   In the light of this, we'd better not open the shop.

Old Woman   Of course, if everything else is closed. It's lucky we have enough food.

Daughter   They haven't delivered the paper for two days.

Old Woman   The paper boy doesn't want to be a hero.

Old Man   There should never be any papers. Although they've got access to all the news, they just publish what shows them in a good light. When I say 'eternity', I mean something that lasts for life. So it's different from what priests think. And an enemy who becomes your friend is always unpleasant. Nothing in life is guaranteed by the same oaths; believe me.

Old Woman   Yes; and many children who have been born have been hidden.

Daughter   Do you think so, Mrs Neptunia?

Old Woman   Ah, if you don't believe me, you won't stand any chance in life!

Old Man   I've already told her that.

Daughter   If you want me to believe you . . .

Old Woman   There are so many people who believe one thing but say another.

Old Man   I'm looking forward to reading what the papers are going to say about the snowfall. I'm sure they'll say that everything was fine and that the emergency services – which we can't see anywhere now – have been as efficient as necessary. They'll say something like 'Efficient performance of the emergency services'. In other words, the authorities will revel in the glory. You'll see.

Daughter   Father, why won't you let me go out?

Old Woman   Do you want to kill yourself?

Old Man (*to the* **Old Woman**) We don't even have any
water.

Old Woman We don't either.

Old Man Why should we be grateful to the town
council?

Old Woman It must be getting colder. (*She rubs her hands
together.*) Well, yesterday we had water for just an instant, but
it looked like mud.

Old Man As you can see, we're living in a hopeless city.
Everything that's unexpected causes a disaster.

Old Woman I can't even listen to the radio.

Daughter I'm going upstairs to see if there's any water.

Old Man Lola, do you remember the story about pigeons
I told you yesterday?

Daughter They weren't pigeons, they were sparrows.

Old Man Well, sparrows then.

Daughter If we were as many as we are, half of us,
double the third of us, you, your brother, your father and
your mother, your son and your daughter, we'd be exactly a
hundred and ten.

Old Woman What?

Old Man Yes, woman, because there were forty-eight
sparrows.

Daughter (*to the* **Old Woman**) Don't you understand?

Old Woman No, I don't.

Old Man Listen: there are forty-eight; half of them is
twenty-four; double the third makes thirty-two; and you,
your brother, your father, your mother, your son and your
daughter, in other words six, gives a total of a hundred and
ten.

Old Woman   Bah, arithmetic! That won't make you famous. Being good at arithmetic won't stop us making a single mistake, Tony.

Old Man   But . . .

Old Woman   People who are really wise play down this knowledge, because the ones who know it don't value wisdom.

Old Man   Doesn't arguing, perhaps, show wisdom?

Old Woman   Yes, but you can't find wisdom in words.

Old Man   And staying weak means being strong?

Old Woman   Yes, it does.

Daughter   Well, I'm going to see if there's any water. (*She exits.*)

Old Man   At heart I'm a pacifist.

Old Woman   He who knows names should know that there are things that can't be named.

Old Man   Why are you telling me this?

Old Woman   Because before being weak you have to be strong.

Old Man   Thinking about it, you're right.

Old Woman   Of course, you mortal man.

Old Man   Neptunia, these ideas are new to me, but you seem to have thought about them a lot, haven't you?

Old Woman   Bah! I don't think they're important. I just repeat them, as if somebody were whispering them in my ear.

Old Man   And do you think other people think like that?

Old Woman   I don't think there are people like that.

Old Man   Have you had a happy marriage?

Old Woman   And where did you find your ring?

Old Man   Do you think I'm that nasty?

Old Woman   I might be breathless, but I know I'm on the right track.

Old Man   It's getting cold in here. (*He rubs his hands together.*)

Old Woman   My father was always suspicious of you.

Old Man   But you put up with it.

Old Woman   Bah! There's no point in talking about that now. What I do know is that we should have talked about it before. I know it's like I say it is. The pain doesn't start now.

Old Man   You know I've spoken highly of your son. He's a reliable boy. And I think he knows what he wants. Although in this life nothing stays the same.

Old Woman   Often it's a woman who makes things change.

Old Man   You and me, we've always been on the same side. (*Darkness.*)

Old Woman   Not again! How pathetic! That takes the biscuit!

Old Man (*has lit the candle*)   That's what wisdom's about.

Old Woman   We're getting left behind.

Old Man   Military service should be abolished.

Old Woman   I can't believe such things are going on nowadays!

Old Man   My daughter has turned out just as I wanted her to.

Old Woman   Yes, she has. I like listening to her saying good things about you.

Old Man   In her way, she's very peaceful. And, up to now, she can remember everything. She remembers all the details and knows there are some streets which lead nowhere. Her memory is perfect. I think she isn't going to be a housewife all her life.

Old Woman   And what makes you think she would have stayed at home anyway?

Old Man   As far as I'm concerned . . . (*The lights come on.*) About time too! (*He puts the candle out.*)

Old Woman   I know for sure that honest people are going to be victims of the snow.

Old Man   Sometimes I feel like emigrating to another country.

Old Woman   Wherever anybody sits down to eat, the tablecloth ends up dirty.

Old Man   Nowadays even going for a walk can be dangerous.

Old Woman   We should be careful!

Old Man   And there are so many impostors around!

Old Woman   And aren't you one of them?

Old Man   Me?

Old Woman   You aren't any good at it.

Old Man   Sometimes I think I'm the only one who hasn't been an impostor.

Old Woman   Well, it makes no difference.

Old Man   You're right: they just play by the rules.

Old Woman (*the lights go out again*)   Damn it! God!

Old Man   We'll never earn enough for all these candles. (*He lights it.*)

Old Woman   You bet we won't!

Old Man   I don't think it can go on either.

Old Woman   Why doesn't this city have another name?

Old Man   In my opinion, the problems are going to spread. Your son told me that, because of the snowfall, the roof of a warehouse collapsed where they were keeping five hundred thousand kilos of potatoes.

Old Woman   See? We should try to clear the snow off our roof as soon as possible. Johnny shouldn't have gone out. I wonder what he's doing in the street. A lot of people are going to fall over.

Old Man   If you need milk, I've got some spare bottles.

Old Woman   Thank you; but I still have some; by pure chance, I'd just bought some.

Old Man   We're done for if this goes on for long.

Old Woman   It seems as if we're in a hurry to go on living.

Old Man   It looks like it.

Old Woman   Everything has changed so much in just two days!

Old Man   It looks as if our town has changed its colour and its appearance.

Old Woman   As you can see, Tony, we're nothing!

Old Man   The weather isn't everything.

Old Woman   That's because of the damn bombs they drop to kill our sons and daughters.

Old Man   You're absolutely right. (*The lights come on.*) At last! (*He puts the candle out.*) Let's see how long they'll stay on.

Old Woman   Look, here comes your daughter. (*The* **Daughter** *enters.*)

Daughter   We haven't got any water yet.

Old Woman   They aren't in any great hurry.

Daughter   There's a load of dishes to be washed up.

Old Man   Huh! It's not worth talking about that again.

Daughter   I don't know what sort of a country we're in.

Old Woman   Whatever you say Lola, when the snow freezes, it'll be a lot worse.

Old Man   The newspaper's only going to print unimportant stories.

Daughter   And the real facts are under our very noses.

Old Woman   I don't know who could be interested in my hands. (*She rubs her hands together.*)

Old Man   Don't exaggerate, Neptunia, even servants fall in love.

Daughter (*darkness*)   Oh! Here we go again!

Old Man   Here we go again! (*He lights the candle again.*)

Old Woman   Damn it!

Old Man   As soon as the lights come on, they go off again.

Old Woman   Poor us!

Daughter   I don't understand why it's taking so long!

Old Woman   We're lucky to have candles.

Daughter   There's still a box left.

Old Man   I always try to take precautions. (*To the* **Old Woman**.) Aren't you going to thank me, girl?

Old Woman   You've always done everything in a rush.

Daughter   Is that true?

Old Man (*to the* **Old Woman**)   Is that the only thing you can say about me?

Old Woman   By the way, it must be late.

Daughter   There's nothing like travelling in your imagination.

Old Man   Yes, it must be late.

Old Woman   Don't say that to calm me down.

Old Man   Don't forget you have a son.

Daughter   Yes.

Old Woman   But I don't feel guilty for anything I've done.

Daughter (*pause*)   And now, what can I do?

Old Woman   It's better to sell something than to lose it.

Daughter   I wanted to go to the cinema.

Old Woman   Living on our poor income.

Old Man   Let's hope spring will be better.

Daughter   Now I'd like to put on a disguise.

Old Man (*light*)   They've fixed it! (*He blows out the candle.*) Bah!

Daughter   If every day was like today . . .

Old Woman   I'm already fed up with being on stage. I'm going to lock myself in the kitchen, now that there's light. (*While she exits.*) Make yourself at home.

Old Man   OK, girl. (*After a pause.*) Lola.

Daughter   Yes, father?

Old Man   Is it very cold upstairs?

Daughter   Yes, since we've run out of oil . . .

Old Man   Politicians only think about their own stomachs.

Daughter   These days the queues are unbearable!

Old Man   You're telling me.

Daughter   The telephone doesn't work either.

Old Man   I'd prefer to fight.

Daughter   I've tried phoning the shop.

Old Man   Of course, it must be closed. Nobody would go out on a day like this!

Daughter   How do you think I look?

Old Man   Fine. And how do you think I look?

Daughter   Fine.

Old Man   I'm not saying the opposite.

Daughter   Don't you think everything that's happening is rather odd?

Old Man   No; the weather men always get it wrong.

Daughter   Yes, you've already said that.

Old Man   Have I? Sometimes when I'm talking, it seems as if I don't know the meaning of words.

Daughter   Then you'd better shut up.

Old Man (*laughs. Pause*)   The lights haven't gone out yet.

Daughter   But do you think there haven't been any accidents?

Old Man   I don't know.

Daughter   Why must these tragedies happen?

Old Man   My daughter, nature is deaf and indifferent.

Daughter   Yes, it is.

Old Man   You have to bear in mind that in nature there's neither justice nor compassion for anything; things happen and that's all there is to it.

Daughter   And did someone create nature?

Old Man I don't think so.

Daughter And what about religions?

Old Man They've been made up by human minds. The way they've manipulated words!

Daughter The world is small, but it makes a fair racket!

Old Man Culture is just a game of lazing about and doing nothing.

Daughter Not necessarily.

Old Man When those at the top are pretty blasé about it.

Daughter Maybe you're right.

Son (*enters while brushing the snow from his coat*) I'd better not go out while this lasts . . .

Daughter About time! You're getting everything wet. Take your coat off.

Son (*turns his back and unbuttons his coat*) Come on: help me.

Old Man (*while the* **Daughter** *takes the* **Son**'*s coat off him*) I can see you're having a good time going in and out.

Son On the street the snow is one and a half metres deep.

Daughter And we still haven't got any water.

Son People say everything's come to a standstill in the city centre too.

Daughter I can understand that we're not prepared for snowfalls here, and especially one like this. (*To the* **Son**.) Your mother says she doesn't remember anything like it.

Old Man It must have been about fifty years ago, when we had a bad time of it as well. But it was more bearable. And I remember we had water to wash our feet. The town council acted more and talked less. People should protest; that's what I think!

Son You don't have to tell me that!

Old Man   And everything we export?

Son   In my opinion, each public services office should have a snow plough, at least. And a group of people ready to act in case of emergencies. They should also order the shops to open where tyre chains and shovels are sold.

Old Man   They aren't interested in that. They're incapable of doing anything.

Daughter (*has left the* **Son***'s coat on a chair*)   Aren't you cold, Johnny?

Son   No, Lola, why?

Daughter   Will you follow my advice? Will you do what I tell you?

Son   What advice?

Old Man   Of course he will, it's for his own good, isn't it?

Daughter   Don't go out again today.

Old Man   It's for your own good.

Son   Yes: the city isn't looking very nice.

Old Man (*rubbing his hands together*)   My God! It's really cold. (*He paces up and down.*)

Daughter (*to the* **Son**)   Do you like lions?

Son   Are you giving me orders?

Daughter   Do you like deer?

Son   Are you using me as a prop?

Daughter   Do you like birds?

Son   Are these the only sorts of questions you can ask me?

Old Man   I prefer fighting. (*He is still walking up and down, rubbing his hands together.*)

Daughter   Do you like talking about this with me?

Son   Do you think I'm good at it?

Daughter   Yes, of course, Johnny.

Son   Is my mother out?

Daughter   She's in the kitchen.

Old Man   The lights haven't gone out yet. If the roof doesn't fall in, everything will be all right.

Daughter   I'd like a little dog which could learn to read and write.

Son   When the sun rises, it rises for everybody.

Old Man   I'd never have imagined that in my old age the snow would become a problem and something to worry about. I've always been so fond of snowy landscapes!

Daughter   Promises never come true.

Son   The fog isn't thick enough to be a problem.

Old Man (*to the* **Daughter**)   You never put any make-up on, do you?

Daughter   If I were an actress, no character would fit me. (*To the* **Son**.) What about you?

Son   I don't know, that's not my strong point.

Old Man   The hair around the temples and forehead is the first to go white.

Son (*to the* **Daughter**)   Wouldn't you like to build a snowman?

Daughter   Do you think we'd manage it?

Old Man   What should we do to clear the snow?

Son   We shouldn't keep the salt in salt cellars.

Old Man   You're right. A couple of lorries salting the streets would be a great help in clearing it. The town council would really disappoint all of us.

Daughter   When you clear the snow off the terrace roof, I'll go out to the street to make sure nobody gets hurt.

Son   I think the lights are out in Badalona.

Daughter   Don't mention the lights, please . . . (*She looks at the light deliberately.*)

Old Man   Yes. I think we should clear the snow off the roof.

Son   We run the risk of having to throw it into the street.

Old Man   If only it'd rain! It would solve everything.

Daughter (*to the* **Son**)   You see how it's dangerous to be out in the street?

Old Man   I'm sure the town councillors have stayed at home today.

Son   It's so absurd.

Daughter   They're in such a hurry to make money!

Old Man   You're saying what I've said already.

Son   And the post hasn't been collected either.

Old Man   It's so sad to depend on people you hate!

Son   And the roads have been cut off.

Old Man   I'm going out on the roof.

Daughter   Make sure you don't throw snow on to the parked cars.

Son   I'll be there to help you in a minute. (*The* **Old Man** *exits.*)

Daughter (*shouting*)   Put your hat and scarf on!

Son   Lola, your intonation isn't very good.

Daughter   Whenever I write a name, I'd always like to underline it.

Son   When I write, I pay more attention to punctuation.

Daughter   I'd like to soften my voice.

Son   And the pauses, yes, the pauses.

Daughter   Why don't we talk in rhymes?

Son   Reciting the whole time?

Daughter   Do you think you need many skills?

Son   Nobody would be able to say everything they think.

Daughter   Do you think they do now?

Son   We'd all be like actors.

Daughter   And aren't we like them now? Eh?

Son   Most actors talk in a more affected voice.

Daughter   Don't you think it's better to raise your voice than hold a conversation on stage in a natural way?

Son   I think every play should have its own intonation. Well, I don't really know, theatre is not my strong point.

Daughter   I don't like annoying unhappy people either.

Son   Your voice seems to be getting stronger now. (*He pinches her nose.*)

Daughter   Everything you touch turns to fire.

Son   I see you're not running away.

Daughter   I always dream about a garden gate.

Son   And does it welcome you?

Daughter   You can see I'm not running away.

Son   I like the length of your pauses and I like . . . (*Darkness.*)

Daughter   Again! Damn it!

Son   Are your hands here?

Daughter   Yes.

Son   I like it when you go shopping.

Daughter   Have you ever seen me shopping?

Son   Yes.

Daughter   Isn't my voice softer now?

Son   And your pauses are great.

Daughter   I like the art of singing. If people sang more often, their intonation would be correct.

Son   And would you prefer people to sing instead of talk?

Daughter   Why not, on Sunday afternoons?

Son (*laughs*)   That's a good one!

Daughter   Why have you let go of my hands? Come on, hold me. That's it; now you're doing what I want.

Son   Nothing could be easier for me; believe me. (*He laughs.*)

Daughter   What's the matter with you, Johnny?

Son   Do you want me to sing?

Daughter   No, no.

Son   Whatever you want.

Daughter   Whatever you want, not whatever I want.

Son   Don't you get tired in the dark?

Daughter   Do I happen to be running away from you?

Son   Say 'shadow'.

Daughter   Sha-dow. (*The lights come on.*) Oh!

Son (*they stand still, holding hands*)   Come on, say 'shadow'.

Daughter   Sha-dow.

Son   Yes; you hardly move your mouth. Your 'o' is lovely, round and dark.

Daughter   You're interested, aren't you?

Son   I think I'll never be able to tell you off.

Daughter (*laughs*)   And following you, I'll never get tired.

Son   No. I'll never be the one to tell you off.

Daughter   What if I sometimes deserve it . . .

Son   What did you say: 'Whatever I want and not whatever you want'? . . .

Daughter   Whatever you want and not whatever I want.

Son   And, by the by, I'll keep you in touch with this messy world.

Daughter   Remember, my father is waiting for you on the roof.

Son   Oh, yes!

Daughter   Johnny. (*She stares at him.*) Is everything you're insinuating true?

Son (*with affection*)   Yes, it's true that every day I need you more.

Daughter (*very excited*)   I thought I'd go mad when you told me that, but I'm not deeply moved. I don't know why.

Son   If there's another man . . .

Daughter   No, no; everything is perfect when I'm with you. It's time you knew that as well.

Son   I know, because I know you.

Daughter   Do you?

Son   Remember I've promised you the moon.

Daughter   You've already given it to me, my star. (*She hugs him.*)

Son   And a gold ring for your little finger. (*He kisses her finger.*)

Daughter   I don't mind if it's made of tin.

Son   As you can see, we'll live comfortably.

Daughter   Johnny, I know I'll make you happy.

Son   I don't doubt that.

Daughter   Just as happy as I am.

*The **Son** kisses her on the forehead.*

Daughter (*returns the kiss*)   The first one.

Son   The first one.

Daughter   Thank you!

Son   Why? Come on! Let's go to the roof and clear the snow. (*They exit holding hands.*)

Quick curtain.

Act Two

White curtain. On stage, the **First Old Woman**, *the* **Second Old Woman** *and the* **Old Man**, *seated.*

First Old Woman   And in the picture, the dog was painted red.

Second Old Woman   That's ridiculous!

First Old Woman   I'll repeat it because I see you don't believe me.

Old Man   Yes, I do.

First Old Woman   And, apparently, somebody paid a lot for the picture: thousands. At least. Even if it had been a present, I wouldn't have wanted it in my home.

Second Old Woman   And who's kidnapped that picture?

First Old Woman   I'm not sure: I don't know them.

Old Man   It's rather strange you don't know them.

Second Old Woman   And can't you tell me the exact price?

First Old Woman   I'm not sure; I don't know anything about them. A fortune.

Second Old Woman   I agree with you – there are some silly people around.

Old Man (*to the* **First Old Woman**)   If you don't mind, I'd like to ask you a few questions.

First Old Woman   Go on then, Ray. Give me a going over. You aren't my enemy.

Second Old Woman (*laughs*)   Of course he's not!

First Old Woman   And I hope to God we'll never be enemies.

Second Old Woman   That's what the aristocracy should
be: friendship.

First Old Woman   If we weren't well thought of, I'd
start crying.

Second Old Woman   We're well thought of and also
highly regarded, don't you know!

First Old Woman   Of course we are!

Second Old Woman   And do you think, Bernadette,
that the people who bought the picture come from a good
family?

First Old Woman   Yes I do, Rufina.

Old Man \ Are you going to let me speak or aren't you?

Second Old Woman   What do you think, Bernadette,
should we let him speak? (*The old women laugh.*)

Old Man (*clears his throat*)   I think there are things that
always come back. That's the only answer I can give to what
we were talking about before. Buying and selling will always
be necessary. And there will always be sewing machines.

Second Old Woman   And umbrellas!

First Old Woman   And lotteries for charity!

Second Old Woman   And alarm clocks!

First Old Woman   And coffee pots!

Second Old Woman   And gold watches!

First Old Woman   And oil heaters!

Second Old Woman   And top hats and boots!

First Old Woman   And pianolas!

Old Man   Please shut up! That's exactly what I meant.
Do you two remember how to dance the rigadoon?

First Old Woman   It's not at all like the polka . . .

Second Old Woman   Isn't it?

Old Man   Isn't it what?

Second Old Woman   I'm not very good at remembering things.

First Old Woman   Oh, Ray, you danced the rigadoon like a king!

Old Man   But my hernia was hell.

Second Old Woman   But you had an operation, didn't you?

Old Man   Yes, I did, just before my wife died.

First Old Woman   I don't like the dances in fashion nowadays. They're immoral and depraved. They're so stupidly chaotic! (*She stands up.*) Will you excuse me for just a moment? (*She exits.*)

Second Old Woman   One has to be so patient in life!

Old Man   Do you still eat dessert?

Second Old Woman   Yes: I keep it in a console.

Old Man   I can't eat dessert any more; it gives me toothache.

Second Old Woman   The thing is I don't have any teeth any more. As you know, my Godfried, may he rest in peace, was a dentist. And he couldn't live without me. He always ordered me about and used me as a patient in the summer, when he didn't have much work.

Old Man (*aside, to the audience*)   All women are like that.

Second Old Woman   He used to say I had a fine figure. And other things, well, enough said . . .

Old Man   Once upon a time, evening parties were the fashion: once a week, after dinner.

Second Old Woman   Oh, yes! That's how I met my Godfried, may he rest in peace. We always had evening parties at home.

Old Man   And how did you give out the invitations?

Second Old Woman   We didn't give them out. We invited our friends by word of mouth.

Old Man   Not in our house. I sent out letters at the beginning of every season inviting them to all the parties we were going to have. It was more practical.

Second Old Woman   Yes, of course, but since my Godfried, may he . . .

Old Man (*annoyed*)   Yes, yes . . . 'rest in peace' . . .

Second Old Woman   . . . since he was a dentist . . .

First Old Woman (*returns*)   What's that about a dentist?

Second Old Woman   My Godfried, may he rest in peace, was a dentist.

Old Man   Bah!

First Old Woman   Oh, yes! Of course! He took quite a few of my teeth out.

Second Old Woman   Did he?

Old Man   Did he what?

Second Old Woman   My Godfried . . .

Old Man   Yes, yes; OK, OK . . .

Second Old Woman   . . . may he rest in peace, was a good dentist.

First Old Woman   Ray.

Old Man   What do you want, young lady?

First Old Woman   How much do you want for it?

Old Man   I'll tell you, since you insist.

Second Old Woman   So, are you going to sell it to her?

Old Man (*to the* **First Old Woman**)   I've already told you that the wardrobe has three sections, it's in Louis XVI style, with a mirror in the middle.

First Old Woman   And is it very high?

Old Man   Oh, yes! And the drawers are very wide.

First Old Woman   And what colour is it?

Old Man   Blue, light blue. And the doors have Marie Antoinette's favourite musical instruments embossed on them.

Second Old Woman   Which ones?

Old Man   The drum, a flute and the castanets. (*To the* **First Old Woman**.) You'll thank me if you buy it.

First Old Woman   And is it in good condition?

Old Man   It's completely new, believe me.

Second Old Woman   And have you only got one?

First Old Woman   Why? Would you like one too?

Second Old Woman   I don't know; maybe I'd put it in the bedroom, next to the chest of drawers. It would go well there, wouldn't it? You said it's Louis XVI, didn't you?

Old Man   Exactly.

Second Old Woman   I like that style.

First Old Woman (*to the* **Second Old Woman**)   And you knew he was selling the wardrobe and you hid it from me, Rufina, eh?

Second Old Woman   I didn't, Bernadette.

First Old Woman   Because you'd be capable of it.

Old Man   But I didn't, Bernadette.

Second Old Woman (*to the* **First Old Woman**)   You think I'd be capable of it, just because *you* would do it to me.

First Old Woman   Me?

Old Man   Bah, that's enough, good girls. The rag-and-bone man told me it's a genuine piece of furniture and, therefore, as I'm not interested in it, he asked me to try to find a good buyer. That's why it occurred to me. That doesn't mean you have to follow my advice.

First Old Woman   And why aren't you interested in it?

Old Man   I've already got enough furniture!

Second Old Woman   When I think about it, I've got too much furniture as well, because there are only the two of us. My health has ruined my life!

First Old Woman   How is your niece doing?

Second Old Woman   She doesn't have any problems . . . She was born with a silver spoon in her mouth. She spends the whole day scraping her violin.

First Old Woman   She should start thinking about marriage.

Second Old Woman   Forget it: she's no good at choosing a partner. She just goes on scraping away!

First Old Woman (*to the* **Old Man**)   Wasn't the violin one of Marie Antoinette's favourite instruments?

Old Man   The viola; I'd forgotten. And there are also flowery bows embossed on the doors.

Second Old Woman   Good gracious, my God, what a wardrobe!

Old Man (*to the* **First Old Woman**)   It's been ages since I wanted to tell you, and I kept forgetting.

First Old Woman   Then perhaps it won't be there any more.

Old Man   For my part, I'll let you know.

First Old Woman   I've been looking for a piece of furniture like that for the bedroom next to the sitting-room for some time now. Marianne has a strong sense of duty!

Second Old Woman   You treat that girl as if she were your own daughter.

First Old Woman   Isn't that understandable for a woman of my age living alone?

Second Old Woman   As long as she doesn't cause any trouble.

First Old Woman   Bah! Don't be so pessimistic.

Old Man   She always has the meals ready on time, I'll say that for her.

Second Old Woman   I'm only worried about you.

First Old Woman   I prefer not to have to deal with tenant farmers.

Old Man   Yes, you're right. They're the ones who are the fullest and the hungriest.

Second Old Woman   I'm too old to sit in stage boxes.

First Old Woman   If I adopt her, she'll inherit everything. (*She exits.*)

Second Old Woman   Marianne'll be lucky if she adopts her.

Old Man   Let's just hope this turns out for the best.

Second Old Woman   Why not take advantage of the situation?

Old Man   Yes, why not?

Second Old Woman   Those poor village people can even end up living as well as we do.

Old Man   If they deserve it . . .

Second Old Woman   But I'm upset by their anger against us.

Old Man   Firstly, they have to carry our buckets.

Second Old Woman   But, sometimes, they get worked up and do stupid things. They're fond of revolutions.

Old Man   Bah! If they're satisfied, they won't give them a thought. The buckets they carry can also be used to put a fire out. (*He laughs.*)

Second Old Woman   Maybe: you probably know better than I do.

Old Man   You have to know people.

Second Old Woman   It's just that all too often they come to cause trouble.

Old Man   Bah! The boss is always the boss.

Second Old Woman   Heaven forbid that we should end up with our heads in baskets again, just like they did in France.

Old Man   That's why it's so important to make them carry good buckets.

Second Old Woman   And if they don't like them?

Old Man   Then – and only then – the stick.

Second Old Woman   Ah! Can't you see that, in the end, you agree with me?

Old Man   OK: a stick or a thump with a bucket. (*He laughs.*) Well, I've already retired from business. I think I deserve it, don't I? For my part, I always did my best. The business had had it. I was lucky with the 1914 war. You see? That was also provoked by people who only wanted to cause trouble. They always end up getting booted out. If they don't run away by themselves first.

Second Old Woman   Yes, the boss is always the boss, isn't he?

Old Man   In short: I'm only here to have a good time.

First Old Woman (*comes back*)   You should see how much Shilling eats! He's so proud of his new collar!

Second Old Woman   Which kind did you buy, one with a chain?

First Old Woman   One of the best around: and I got his name and address engraved on it so he doesn't get lost. Although he always goes for a walk with Marianne. And she's very cautious. He's the most beautiful little dog in the world.

Old Man   Well, well!

Second Old Woman   You don't like animals very much, Ray, do you? I don't agree with you on that point.

Old Man   Anyone who wants a little animal without having a garden has no more common sense than the little animal he wants.

Second Old Woman   You see? I do agree with you on that point.

First Old Woman   But I have a terraced roof and lots of other things.

Old Man   Cats and dogs make too much of a racket inside a home.

First Old Woman   But they're so good at keeping you company! And they're more grateful than people.

Old Man   Of course, because you don't expect anything from them, and you do from people. Everything they give you is unexpected.

Second Old Woman   I do agree with you on that point.

First Old Woman   My dear, there are people who are capable of committing any infamy.

Old Man   Yes, yes; that isn't a miracle. It's a long time since I believed in anybody; it makes no difference whether they take my side or not. As soon as you help someone they take advantage of you.

Second Old Woman   Yes, that's true.

First Old Woman   In this world you've got to beat people until your stick breaks.

Second Old Woman   We were speaking about that earlier, weren't we?

Old Man   Oh, yes! We already know how everything's going.

First Old Woman   *I* don't even know how old I am: it's always been the same and always will be.

Second Old Woman   I agree with you, Bernadette; I don't want favours from anybody, even if I'm on the receiving end. You only need to be pleasant at the right time.

Old Man (*stands up*)   Up we get!

First Old Woman   Are you late?

Old Man   Me? No; I assure you I congratulate you on everything. (*He exits.*)

Second Old Woman   I think there's something wrong with Ray.

First Old Woman   Him? He's got everything he needs!

Second Old Woman   Then he's not quite sure what he wants.

First Old Woman   Before you can say that, you need to be with him all the time.

Second Old Woman   God forbid! I only mean that I think he's a bit skinny.

First Old Woman   Yes, maybe he is a bit thinner, but at his age it's better to be thin.

Second Old Woman   Or perhaps his cook isn't very good.

First Old Woman   At certain times of life we shouldn't eat a lot.

Second Old Woman   Yes; but when all's said and done, I'm not the only one to notice he's gone downhill. You have too, haven't you?

First Old Woman   Yes; but I don't know if he's suffering from any illness. He once had a hernia operation . . . but that was years ago.

Second Old Woman   That's men's main defect.

First Old Woman   What? Having a hernia operation? My husband didn't have a hernia; well, not as far as I know.

Second Old Woman   No; I mean that men's main defect is doing and undoing things too quickly. Sometimes, my Godfried's face, may he still rest in peace, wasn't as I wanted it to be. He looked all depressed.

First Old Woman   My husband wasn't. He always did everything he wanted.

Second Old Woman   But going back to what we were saying: I don't mind saying that Ray doesn't look sure about what he's doing. I mean he asks and doesn't answer. And he answers without asking.

First Old Woman   I don't know: I only give him what he asks me for.

Second Old Woman   And they say Ray doesn't want to wear glasses and that harms his eyes.

First Old Woman   But he doesn't do any tiring jobs; he's spent all his life giving orders.

Second Old Woman   I'm only telling you what people say.

First Old Woman   He and I both go to the same doctor.

Second Old Woman   My doctor seems to be soft in the head.

First Old Woman   What can I say? Why do you still go to him, then? . . .

Second Old Woman   Actually I need to see him now, because he has to check my blood pressure.

First Old Woman   I've got low blood pressure. What about you? Don't you feel well?

Second Old Woman   Maybe I've got too much saliva; but that's not unnatural, is it?

First Old Woman   I have to be careful with my blood pressure. It suddenly goes up.

Second Old Woman   Well, I've always got too much saliva.

First Old Woman   And what does the doctor say?

Second Old Woman   Can I talk to you in complete confidence? (*Whispering.*) Ray's feet smell awful.

First Old Woman   Come off it!

Second Old Woman   Pay close attention.

First Old Woman   I don't know; I don't tend to want to pay any attention to that sort of thing.

Second Old Woman   You told me I could talk to you in complete confidence.

First Old Woman   You can, you can.

Old Man (*comes back*)   How is it possible for some people to dream without being asleep?

First Old Woman (*to the* **Second Old Woman**, *aside*) Pay close attention!

Old Man   How is it possible . . .

Second Old Woman (*to the* **First Old Woman**, *aside*) What?

First Old Woman (*aside*)   His feet . . .

Old Man   I never dream.

First Old Woman   They say everybody dreams.

Old Man   Well, I don't.

Second Old Woman (*discreetly lets her handkerchief fall at the* **Old Man***'s feet*)   Ah! I'm sorry, Ray. (*To the* **First Old Woman**.) Can you pick that up for me, Bernadette?

First Old Woman   Me?

Old Man (*picks up the handkerchief*)   Here you are, Rufina.

Second Old Woman   Thank you! (*She contemptuously looks at the* **First Old Woman**, *who did not understand her intention*.)

Old Man   Don't mention it, my dear.

First Old Woman   By the way . . . maybe I'm wrong, but don't you think the heating is on too high?

Second Old Woman   I don't know, as I'm wearing wool . . .

First Old Woman   And what about you, Ray?

Old Man   I think it's all right.

Second Old Woman   Let me see if your hands are cold? (*She touches his hands*.) You're wrong not to wear glasses.

Old Man   That's it! Now you really are talking for the sake of it.

First Old Woman   Apparently you read a lot, is that right?

Old Man   Every day I read a detective story before going to bed.

Second Old Woman (*to the* **First Old Woman**, *deliberately*)   You see? (*To the* **Old Man**.) Another reason why you should wear glasses.

Old Man   Bah! When I'm at home, I think about the streets; and when I'm on the streets, I think about home.

Second Old Woman (*aside, to the* **First Old Woman**)   You see? Did you hear that?

First Old Woman (*worried about her idea*)   I don't know what to think about the heating.

Second Old Woman   Nowadays people don't fall in love.

First Old Woman (*exiting*)   This is an omen!

Second Old Woman   You're very quiet.

Old Man   I think the heating is fine.

Second Old Woman   Nowadays, people are too tolerant when others live together.

Old Man   Perhaps they are.

Second Old Woman   When I married, I didn't know anything about men. I'd never stepped outside my parents' house. Nowadays girls are bad pearls. They take too many liberties, by day and by night. And there's no more poetry. I remember how excited I got when I went up to my fiancé and grabbed his cloak. I'm telling the truth.

Old Man   OK, OK, Rufina. I don't need to know all this.

Second Old Woman   When I went to bed, my teeth were chattering.

Old Man   You were overdoing it a bit as well.

Second Old Woman   Oh, Ray! Everybody shows off what they've got.

Old Man   As long as there aren't any excesses.

Second Old Woman   But I'm happy I don't have a young child.

Old Man   At one time I was really interested in weapons. Even though my father had enough money to get me out of military service. It was called 'cash redemption'. The fact is I didn't leave home.

Second Old Woman   And that was the right thing to do. Why should the rich mix with the poor? The poor are more suited to being soldiers. They're used to poverty and hardship.

Old Man   My father soon taught me how to run our business. He was one of those who belonged to the 'nobility of commerce', as it was then called.

First Old Woman (*enters*)   Everything's all right.

Second Old Woman   So you're not worried now?

First Old Woman   Where do *you* buy your cheese?

Second Old Woman   My cheese?

First Old Woman   Yes.

Second Old Woman   It's a shame the cheese they've got now isn't any better than the cheese they used to have.

Old Man   Is that really true?

First Old Woman   I like cheese a lot. I don't know: eating cheese gives me a feeling of freedom.

Second Old Woman   And you're asking where I buy it?

First Old Woman   If you want, just give me an idea.

Second Old Woman   Of all cheeses, Camembert is my favourite.

Old Man I like refined Gruyère.

Second Old Woman Some people like it with worms and fungus inside.

First Old Woman I thought you'd have to bring worms into it.

Old Man I was also expecting that.

Second Old Woman Well: the best cheese has cream in it, like cheese from Holland. That's really good!

Old Man Oh, choosing a good cheese is an art! At first sight I can never tell good from bad. And I don't think anybody can. I'm always the one who buys the cheese. My cook makes a mess of it.

First Old Woman I like cheese that's made from goat's milk.

Old Man My father used to say there always had to be a good cheese on a rich man's table.

Second Old Woman I agree with you.

First Old Woman Roquefort is made from sheep's milk.

Old Man In Spain we're really behind in cheese production. (*He exits.*)

Second Old Woman How are you feeling today, my girl?

First Old Woman Much the same, as you can see.

Second Old Woman That's how it should be.

First Old Woman (*whispering*) You know, I think Ray dyes his hair?

Second Old Woman Really?

First Old Woman Pay close attention. When he turns round, I think you can see a line at the back of his head.

Besides, he was the one who told me to dye my hair blonde from time to time.

Second Old Woman   He can be so clever sometimes!

First Old Woman   But I pretend not to hear him.

Second Old Woman   He always used to tell me about his problems. Whenever he had the opportunity, of course. Sometimes I didn't feel like listening to him and I pretended to be somebody else. You have to be cunning where men are concerned; otherwise they take too many liberties.

First Old Woman   Everybody knows, in this life, women have to manage in choppy water.

Second Old Woman   When I think that tomorrow I've got to make sticking plasters for the Red Cross, I feel like running away like a little girl. But the Marchioness of Llofriu is such a good friend of mine that if I didn't help her, as she expects me to, she'd kill me. During the war, both of us hid nuns in Sant Hilari. Nobody could ever trace them. Although people from the village sniffed about like dogs.

Old Man (*enters*)   We're really, really behind in cheese production.

First Old Woman (*aside, to the* **Old Man**, *after making a sign to the* **Second Old Woman**)   He who scorns a laid table also scorns work. Come on, Ray, turn round.

Old Man   Me? (*He turns round.*)

First Old Woman (*aside, to the* **Second Old Woman** *pointing to the back of the* **Old Man**'s *neck*)   Don't you think so?

Second Old Woman (*whispering*)   I think you've made it up. The back of his neck is just like ours.

Old Man   Can I turn round again?

First Old Woman   Yes, yes. (*The* **Old Man** *turns round and stares at them, puzzled. Tense pause.*) It's just that . . .

Second Old Woman   It's just that we were saying that . . .
wigs are now back in fashion.

Old Man (*quickly to the* **First Old Woman**)   And why
don't you dye your hair blonde?

Second Old Woman (*to the* **Old Man**)   Don't you like
historical hairstyles?

First Old Woman   Yes, like Marie Antoinette's . . .

Old Man   So, are high wigs back in fashion?

Second Old Woman   Yes, yes, and they can even cover
your ears; and have big white curls hanging down at the
back.

Old Man   To be honest, I haven't seen any.

Second Old Woman   I'm sure you will.

Old Man   If only swords were in fashion again, like in the
old days. And hats with feathers in them.

Second Old Woman   You'd be perfect, Ray!

Old Man   I'd dress up like a musketeer and I'd drive
around the city in my car.

Second Old Woman   Bravo!

First Old Woman   Oh, the carnival is forbidden; thank
God we now go straight into Lent.

Old Man   Carnival was such a stupid festival. I didn't
mean that. What I'm talking about is not clowning about on
rooftops.

Second Old Woman (*stands up*)   I'm going to have a
quick wash. (*She exits.*)

Old Man   We can't know what's going to happen to us;
we only know for sure what has already happened to us.

First Old Woman   The Reverend Eulali says we should
decorate the house with a Nativity scene rather than with a

Christmas tree. Don't you agree with him, Ray? It's better to say your prayers in front of a Nativity scene than in front of snowmen, trees and glass balls. Besides, these things are expensive, and then people complain they don't have enough money to live on.

Old Man   Don't worry: you should dye your hair blonde.

First Old Woman   What's wrong with you? Why do you keep on telling me I should dye my hair blonde? You mean you don't dye your hair?

Old Man   Me?

First Old Woman   If you want, I can give you a magic formula. You don't have to hide it from me. Do you think I haven't noticed?

Old Man   If that's what you've seen, then you'd better wear glasses. Dying my hair, me? Do you think I'm so superficial? Tell me.

First Old Woman   Then, why do you want me to dye my hair blonde? Tell me.

Old Man   All women are exactly the same, you can't help it.

First Old Woman   Don't change the subject, you also dress up.

Old Man   Not again!

First Old Woman   I'll give you a roulette wheel for Christmas.

Old Man   What? And what am I going to do with it?

First Old Woman   I'll have more excuses to come and play.

Old Man   Oh, Bernadette, at our age!

First Old Woman   Don't you think Rufina's aged recently?

Old Man   She's not so young any more.

First Old Woman   She's always busy helping the Red Cross and the Marchioness!

Old Man   Yes, I know.

First Old Woman   Does she tell you about that too?

Old Man   Sometimes.

First Old Woman   Next Thursday we're holding a lunch to help poor children locally. Are you coming? They're so grateful to us!

Old Man   I'll be there, standing tall.

First Old Woman   We're going to the same restaurant as last year. It's expensive, but everything is delicious.

Old Man   Do they have good cheese?

First Old Woman   Even Gruyère!

Old Man   Splendid! I don't like a meal without it. Cheese is the touchstone of a good wine and brings out its bouquet.

First Old Woman   You know what? I've decided that for Christmas I'm not going to donate war toys. Children shouldn't get into bad habits.

Old Man   Why? I don't agree with you. Young people have to get used to handling weapons. There might be a war and it won't be such a novelty for them. I mean, we might need them . . .

First Old Woman   Do you think there might be a war?

Old Man   Who knows! The boss is always the boss. And sometimes he has to impose his authority or suffer the consequences. Just remember the revolution; my eyes and your eyes have seen the same things.

First Old Woman   Of course. God wants us to be here, where all the fun is.

Old Man   Exactly! That's what I meant when I said there could be a war.

Second Old Woman (*comes back*)   There are always a thousand excuses in life. (*She sits down.*) I say that because I've just seen a couple hugging and kissing through the window. Of course, they learn that from films . . .

Old Man   So you looked at them. (*He laughs.*)

Second Old Woman   You've got a nerve to tell me such things.

First Old Woman   But Ray is right!

Second Old Woman   You're being so smug today, Bernadette! Have you already spoken to Ray about the wig?

First Old Woman (*quickly*)   Oh, yes! And we've put you on a pedestal!

Old Man (*laughing*)   You're always found out in the end.

Second Old Woman   I don't think I've broken any law. Perhaps the false words I say are not my own. I never make any mistakes over oaths, thank God. Other people can't claim as much. I don't know what you two were talking about just now.

First Old Woman   I can assure you we did not utter a single pompous name.

Old Man (*laughing*)   We're pretty experienced!

Second Old Woman   Something very serious would have to happen before life became unbearable for me. If I wanted to, I could support an army. But the thing is I'm not proud, I have no pretensions, and I don't smoke or drink. Other people we're well acquainted with can't claim as much. I also haven't got any rips in embarrassing places. There's no reason for me to envy anybody either.

Old Man   Oh, don't take it like that, Rufina. We'd be in a right state if we couldn't look out through the skylight.

Second Old Woman   What do I care what other people do! I don't need them at all, thank God, whether they take notice of me or not.

The **First Old Woman** *gets up.*

Old Man   Are you standing up again?

First Old Woman   I think I've got it! (*She exits.*)

Old Man   I still remember when the first Zeppelin went up. It looked like a submarine in the sea. It was built by a German count, a very famous engineer. I remember that a 'Z', an 'R' and a 'l' were painted on it. And, as if that weren't enough, I was in Paris when the first aeroplanes were tested. I was on my honeymoon. A millionaire was staying in front of my hotel. I wonder where he is now.

Second Old Woman   Really?

Old Man   Yes. We looked so alike that people took us for the same person. Then my wife and I went on to Egypt, which is a very dirty country. The postcards my wife bought there must still be at home somewhere. I can't stand all that mess. I've got pictures from all over the world and I know all the best hotels. I know I've been to a lot of countries, but don't ask me what they look like. That's why I've got the postcards.

Second Old Woman   And what's Paris like?

Old Man   Oh! Very big!

Second Old Woman   And do women let you look at them lying in bed? And can you see women half naked on the streets?

Old Man   Perhaps, but I didn't see any. They'd have told me at the hotel.

Second Old Woman   Ah! The furthest I've been is to Sant Hilari. It was my own choice. Foreign men are malicious. I think I'd feel dizzy abroad.

Old Man   In hotels you can find everything: good and bad.

Second Old Woman   I don't deny it, I don't deny it.

First Old Woman (*comes back*)   Yes . . . there.

Second Old Woman   Were you there, Bernadette?

First Old Woman   Yes, it was definitely Shilling. I had left some meat out on the table and this afternoon I thought I'd have to give up my fondness for Marianne. Half the chops had disappeared. And now I've found the bones outside and Shilling wagging his tail.

Second Old Woman   And do you know for sure that it wasn't the girl?

First Old Woman   I'm convinced.

Old Man   That's what we were saying before about little animals, you see?

Second Old Woman   People who are discreet usually like each other.

First Old Woman   Today Marianne wasn't in a very good mood. You know me, I like her to be quiet while I'm talking, and yesterday she was a bit arrogant. I got angry and told her I'd make her go back to the orphanage. Nuns should be capable of love, shouldn't they? But she burst into tears. And today I had this problem with the meat.

Second Old Woman   Yes, dear; giving orders is easy if you have good servants. Girls nowadays behave as if they were victims. They only have to carry out the decisions we take. I wonder where they get the scruples they have.

First Old Woman   They want to be ladies straight away.

Second Old Woman   Those stuck-up little tarts . . .

First Old Woman   Wealth is pretty rare, thank God.

Old Man   Buying and selling are the basis of everything. (*He laughs.*)

First Old Woman   Ray, you're very quiet.

Second Old Woman   You look like you've just fallen off a train.

Old Man   Now I remember, the first Zeppelin flew on the twelfth of October.

First Old Woman   You've already told me that a dozen times, as if I didn't know who you were.

Old Man   When something's worth it, it always has to be repeated.

Second Old Woman   He's also told me that before; and maybe some other time too.

Old Man   You see? She can't even remember.

First Old Woman   And has he also told you about the hotels he knows?

Old Man   Of course, it's the same story.

Second Old Woman   I say 'hello' to everybody who wants me to.

First Old Woman   Oh! We've got so many problems!

Old Man (*stands up*)   We're mortal from head to toe. (*He exits.*)

Second Old Woman   Weren't you going to buy a statue?

First Old Woman   I wanted to have my bust done; but I don't know: I don't trust sculptors.

Second Old Woman   Some of them are old. Or, if not, a young one can do it for you.

First Old Woman   They're very pretentious.

Second Old Woman   They can do it from memory.

First Old Woman   But, then, how would it look anything like me?

Second Old Woman   You can give him a photograph.

First Old Woman   To be honest, I don't think the solution is that easy.

Second Old Woman   Yes, yes, it's obvious.

First Old Woman   Well, I don't think so.

Second Old Woman   No; I meant, it's obvious, the solution isn't easy.

First Old Woman   Then we agree.

Second Old Woman   I'd think the same if I had to have a sculpture done of me.

First Old Woman   You can get very upset in a thousand different ways.

Second Old Woman   I'd certainly do it wearing a coat and hat.

First Old Woman   Would you like some biscuits and a glass of sherry?

Second Old Woman   No. Thank you, Bernadette.

First Old Woman   Suit yourself; if not today, another time.

Second Old Woman   Ah! Do you know what I saw yesterday? A young boy taking his first communion dressed up as a little Civil Guard.

First Old Woman   Really? Come off it!

Second Old Woman   Yes, yes, he was so sweet with his little white gloves, and his little three-cornered hat, and his little rosaries. He looked as though he was wearing his best clothes.

First Old Woman   Really?

Second Old Woman   I'm sure they'd already discussed it with the priest beforehand. I think it's very original.

First Old Woman   Well, I don't; you have to wear your best clothes when you take your first communion. As you can see: the solution is very easy.

Second Old Woman   But the Church can't interfere with people's tastes.

First Old Woman   These questions should be resolved, once and for all. If they're not, just remember what happened in the Second Republic.

Second Old Woman   Oh, yes! Heaven forbid!

First Old Woman   There are things that shouldn't be hidden: if you don't do them, then you'll regret it for the rest of your life. God wants us to be here, where all the fun is. Just remember the revolution. My eyes and your eyes have seen the same things.

Old Man (*rushes in, very upset*)   Enric Borràs is dead!

Second Old Woman   What, Ray?

First Old Woman   That's not possible!

Old Man   He died, face up.

First Old Woman   Enric Borràs, dead?

Second Old Woman   My God, Bernadette!

First Old Woman   Mary, mother of God, Rufina!

Old Man   Yes, how terrible for all of us!

First Old Woman   Good heavens! The great Borràs!

Second Old Woman   Catalan theatre is in mourning!

Old Man   World theatre, you mean!

First Old Woman   My God! This is terrible! Really terrible!

Old Man   Yes it is, yes.

Second Old Woman   Borràs dead!

Old Man   And he died face up.

First Old Woman   But how did it happen?

Second Old Woman   And when?

First Old Woman   Was it some time ago?

Second Old Woman   And where? Tell us.

First Old Woman   Yes, tell us.

Old Man   He died from an attack of uraemia.

First Old Woman   I knew he was ill, but not that ill! . . .

Second Old Woman   I'd also heard he was seriously ill.

Old Man   They say his last words were unintelligible.

First Old Woman   And he used to be such a good actor!

Second Old Woman   My God, what was the poor man trying to say?

Old Man   Apparently, the doctors did all they could to try and save him, but it was useless.

First Old Woman   Poor Borràs, I can still see him on stage. His acting was so good!

Second Old Woman   What a sad piece of news, Mary, mother of God!

Old Man   That's life, you can't do anything about it! In death, we're all equal.

First Old Woman   And do you know when he'll be buried?

Second Old Woman   That's what . . .

Old Man   No, they don't know yet.

First Old Woman   Did he die in Barcelona?

Old Man   Yes, in his home, in 13, Saint Eudald Street, in Vallcarca.

First Old Woman   My God!

Old Man   The great Borràs has left us. Ever since the African war, he's been the best. No one could touch him; precisely when the theatre has been full of the greatest actors.

First Old Woman   I can still see him playing Manelic in *Marta of the Lowlands*.

Old Man   And in *The Great Galeoto* and in *The Mayor of Zalamea*.

Second Old Woman   And in Iglésias's *The Old Folks*.

Old Man   Bah! Iglésias wrote for the plebs.

First Old Woman   I saw Borràs when he came back from Latin America.

Second Old Woman   He always played his parts so well!

Old Man   He had an absolutely phenomenal talent. The theatre has lost one of its greatest actors.

First Old Woman   And how old was he?

Old Man   Almost a hundred. But when he was young, he was already exceptional. He dedicated his whole life to the theatre. When I was a boy, I saw him acting in Badalona; he was still an amateur. I even knew his grandmother. Then we called him 'Little Enric'. I saw him act in many plays. Every Sunday he was the best of the lot. Once he and my father acted together. As you know, my father was very keen on theatre, and, just for fun, I took part as well. I was young, obviously.

First Old Woman   Poor Borràs! Look, I've come out in goose pimples.

Second Old Woman   And me too! My God!

First Old Woman   He acted so well!

Second Old Woman   Yes, he did!

Old Man   To be honest, I really loved him.

First Old Woman   Why should a personality like him go, and not others who aren't needed . . . ?

Second Old Woman   You took the words right out of my mouth, Bernadette.

Old Man   Yes, yes, these things are frightening and it's better not to think about them.

First Old Woman   He was such a great artist!

Second Old Woman   Art can never die.

Old Man   I think it will take me a long time to get used to the fact that Borràs is dead. I can't believe it.

First Old Woman (*to the* **Old Man**)   You'll have to go to his funeral.

Second Old Woman   Just imagine how many people will be there!

Old Man   Of course, of course.

First Old Woman   This is terrible!

Old Man   It's the end of theatre, or worse than that.

Second Old Woman   Just imagine.

Old Man   It's better not to think about the future.

First Old Woman   Everybody has to do the same when facing this sort of situation; if we live long enough.

Old Man   I saw Borràs playing comic roles as well.

First Old Woman   Really?

Old Man   He was very good.

Second Old Woman   A comic role?

Old Man   And I've got a signed photograph of him. His advice was always good. His genius was immeasurable. But it's over, girls.

Curtain.

Act Three

*Clothes shop in a neighbourhood on the outskirts of the city. On stage the **Old Woman**, the **Old Man**, the **Daughter** and the **Shop Assistant**. The counter is covered in fabrics of all colours.*

Shop Assistant (*serving behind the counter*)　This material is ideal for a cheerful guest; you can't deny it. Feel it, it's lovely. If people wore this kind of material, there wouldn't be so many wicked individuals in the world.

Daughter　I think it could be too light.

Old Woman　You mean it won't do?

Old Man (*referring to the **Shop Assistant***)　Don't be so fussy with the young gentleman.

Shop Assistant　We slaves never complain, young man.

Old Woman　I'd love to wear lots of ribbons.

Shop Assistant (*to the **Old Man***)　The demands of my female customers play a role I always defend.

Daughter　Could you show us a more sober one?

Old Woman　Do you think this isn't smart enough? What do you think, Tony?

Old Man　Whatever you want, Neptunia, but hurry up.

Shop Assistant　I'll show you a more sober one: we're not limited to just one style in this shop. (*He looks for another fabric.*) Nowadays bright colours are in fashion, but they already existed in Sophocles's day.

Old Woman (*to the **Daughter***)　Did you hear that?

Daughter　The point about all this is that it shouldn't have an immediate impact and then you get bored with it.

Old Man　You're not a young girl any more, Neptunia. And it's not that I'm complaining.

Shop Assistant   What do you all think of this colour?

Old Woman   I'll look like a round temple in the middle of a town square.

Shop Assistant   Madam, it's high quality, like all of the selection in this shop.

Old Woman   It looks like wool to me.

Old Man   Maybe it is, maybe it isn't.

Shop Assistant   So, you don't like this one, either?

Old Woman   I don't know. What do you think, Lola?

Shop Assistant   Have you ever held this kind of material in your hands? This material isn't unworthy of anybody. (*To the* **Old Man**, *who is keeping out of it*.) Look at it, young man, look at it.

Old Man   Me? Everything looks symmetrical to me.

Shop Assistant   Did you say symmetrical?

Daughter   How much is this one?

Shop Assistant   By the metre? I'll help you work it out. (*To the* **Daughter**.) Is the dress for you, Miss?

Old Man   Good gracious, she's already married.

Shop Assistant   I'm sorry! Is the dress for you, Madam?

Daughter   No. It's someone else's wedding.

Shop Assistant (*to the* **Old Man** *and the* **Old Woman**) Yours, maybe?

Old Man   Yes, that's right, young man. That's what we've decided to do. Haven't we, Neptunia?

Old Woman (*looking at the fabric*)   Yes, of course. What do you think of it, Lola?

Shop Assistant   I can see you've come without any preconceived idea of what you want.

Old Woman   We just want to see different samples.
Don't we, Lola?

Daughter   Of course, Mrs Neptunia.

Old Woman   Goodness gracious, don't call me 'Mrs'
please! Can't you see it makes me look old? That's not what
I need now. You aren't allowed to call me 'Mrs'. My son
has never called your father 'Mr' since you got married. We
have to be on familiar terms.

Shop Assistant (*laughs*)   Of course; some axes are lethal,
aren't they?

Old Woman   Well; what do you think of this material?
Does it suit me?

Daughter   Maybe it should be a bit darker?

Old Woman   You mean even darker? You want to make
me feel old. Just remember, your father must look like the
king of the Greeks next to me.

Shop Assistant   Bravo! (*He applauds.*)

Old Man   Don't say such things, Neptunia.

Old Woman   Goodness gracious, why can't I? It's what I
think. And I'm proud of it.

Daughter   How much is a metre?

Shop Assistant   Let's see: this one is a hundred and fifty
pesetas.

Old Woman   Did you say one hundred and fifty? No, no.
Then, show us another darker one, as Miss Madam says.

Shop Assistant (*takes out another fabric*)   Look: we've also
got this. It's as pretty as the ghost of the night.

Old Woman   I'll look like a woman taken from a cart to
be sacrificed.

Shop Assistant   There's other business to attend to.
This material is the same as the one we've got in the shop

window, at the top of the column. It's a quality fabric.
Living without any honour is ignominious. Sophocles says
so.

Old Woman   You know, I don't like having enemies.

Shop Assistant   You won't have any disasters with this
material.

Old Woman   Thank you. We have noble hearts.

Shop Assistant   I tell you, I don't doubt it, Madam.

Old Woman   What do you think, Lola? Will this material
make me look too old?

Daughter   I think the best would be a fabric between this
one and that one.

Shop Assistant   If you want to see what it looks like on
you . . . (*He unfolds a few metres of the fabric, and the* **Old
Woman** *tries it on her.*) You see?

Old Woman   You were right, Lola. Don't you have
something in between?

Shop Assistant   Then, you want this one. (*He takes out
another fabric.*)

Daughter   I like it.

Old Woman   Yes; with this one I'll look more like myself,
won't I, Tony?

Old Man   It's up to you, it's up to you.

Shop Assistant (*referring to the pile of fabrics he has on the
counter*)   Oh! It looks like there's been a storm on this
counter.

Old Man   You're right, young man, you're right.

Old Woman (*the women are utterly absorbed by the fabrics*)   Do
you mean that . . .

Daughter   I like it better than the other one.

Old Woman (*to the* **Shop Assistant**)   And won't it shrink when it's washed?

Shop Assistant   Why should it shrink? We don't cheat our customers, Madam. Believe me, you won't regret buying this material.

Daughter   What do you think, Neptunia?

Old Woman (*after a pause*)   I don't know why, but I'm not altogether satisfied with it.

Shop Assistant (*looks at the* **Old Man**)   Huh!

Old Man (*aside*)   We can't do anything, that's the way things are . . .

Old Woman   Do you like it, Tony?

Old Man   Of course I do, Neptunia: very much!

Shop Assistant   Believe me, this material has just arrived. The action begins with you.

Old Man (*aside*)   I understand the position you're in, young man.

Shop Assistant (*aside*)   At night, I dream I'm conquering Troy.

Old Woman (*referring to the fabric*)   I don't know what I'll look like when it's a dress.

Daughter   Like a queen.

Old Woman   The solution is for you to show us one with a pattern.

Shop Assistant   Very good, Madam. (*Aside, to the* **Old Man**.) It's enough to try the patience of a saint!

Old Man   I understand you, but we can't do anything.

Old Woman   I'm sorry about this, young man: we won't be long.

Shop Assistant   Thank you, thank you! (*He goes and looks for the sample.*)

Old Woman (*to the* **Old Man**)   They've got quality material here, haven't they?

Old Man   Oh yes!

Old Woman   But to be completely sure, I have to see things with my own eyes.

Daughter   Compared with other shops, they've got twice as much here.

Shop Assistant (*shows them the sample he has been looking for*) Look at this one. As pretty as a well-told story.

Daughter   Yes, yes, we are all witnesses to that.

Old Woman   And is it as pretty at night as it is during the day?

Shop Assistant   This will light up your face.

Old Woman   That's not the best thing for me: it'll show up my wrinkles.

Shop Assistant   It's just a saying. I mean, you'll forget all your problems, because this material is always perfect for special occasions. It's like the prelude to a dream.

Old Woman   Poor old me, yes, I'll look so smart!

Shop Assistant   Look how carefully it's been woven. Look! Feel it! It's been brought here in secret by an oracle.

Old Woman (*to the* **Daughter**)   What do you think, Lola? Shall we go back?

Shop Assistant   Don't go back, now you're here.

Old Woman   You don't need to be afraid of our pride, young man.

Old Man   Of course not!

Daughter   And how much is this one?

Shop Assistant   Twice the price of the other one.

Old Woman   What? That's outrageous!

Shop Assistant   I know what I'm saying, Madam. Twice as expensive, and next week perhaps three times the price. Can't you see all prices are going up? Life is a peaceful shipwreck.

Old Man   That's what's wrong, that's what's wrong.

Shop Assistant   Believe me, I'm all for people living together. But I don't mind if it's a double fight. We all know. Sophocles was a general.

Old Man   I can see, my young man, that you're a dedicated Sophoclean.

Shop Assistant   Oh, yes, sir! And what's more, that's my name. Robert Sophoclean Drill, at your service. I never miss a historical film. Have you ever seen *The Centaurs of Numancia*?

Old Man   No, I haven't.

Shop Assistant   You should, it's well worth it. It's the story of a sacred temple restored by slaves for their fatherland. The ending is really tremendous.

Old Man   It's made up, Mr Sophoclean.

Shop Assistant   The heroes go into action and they never surrender.

Old Woman (*who was waiting for the* **Shop Assistant** *to stop talking*)   On the other hand, we're completely sure we don't want the first one you showed us. I want the green one.

Shop Assistant   The green one?

Old Woman   Yes, sir, the green one.

Daughter   Neptunia, I think you should buy the third one he showed us.

Shop Assistant   Did you say the third one?

Old Woman   No, I don't want it.

Daughter   The grey one suits you better: you'll soon get tired of the green one.

Old Woman   And why should I pretend, if I like the green one best?

Shop Assistant   This happens all the time, ladies.

Old Woman   I'd stake my life on the green one.

Old Man   Do what she says: I think the girl is right.

Old Woman   Why don't you give me a chance?

A **Customer** *enters slowly and remains on one side of the stage.*

Old Man (*to the* **Old Woman**)   My child, don't be like that!

Old Woman   If you've just woken up, that's no way to put your oar in!

Old Man   I've told you what I think.

Old Woman   Neither of you cares what I want!

Daughter   Don't be like that, Neptunia!

Old Man   We're giving you good advice.

Old Woman   No! (*She thumps the counter.*)

Shop Assistant   Nobody's been injured here, ladies and gentlemen.

Old Woman   I don't like staying in the background.

Old Man   This wedding's upsetting you: believe me.

Old Woman   No! (*Another thump.*)

Shop Assistant   Calm down! Nobody's been injured here, ladies and gentlemen.

Daughter   There's no need to take pity on anybody.

Old Woman   Why are you both talking like this?

Old Man   We're not just sowing seeds anywhere.

Shop Assistant   I'm just reporting what I hear.

Old Man   I don't think we're going to buy anything.

Daughter   That's the way I see things as well.

Old Woman (*to the* **Old Man**)   I don't exist any more, I live through you and you don't even appreciate it.

Old Man   I can't see any hand dripping.

Old Woman   The thing is there's nobody who really understands.

Old Man   We should try our best to get on with each other.

Old Woman   I want the green one!

Old Man   Come on, keep your voice down.

Daughter   But . . .

Old Woman   That's it. That's it. There are no famous asses here worth their salt!

Old Man   All right! Let's go then, because these men have to act.

They all go off. Pause. The **Shop Assistant** *sighs and tidies the counter.*

Shop Assistant (*to the* **Customer**)   Can I help you, sir?

Customer (*goes up to the counter*)   Good afternoon.

Shop Assistant   A very good afternoon to you. How can I help you, sir?

Customer   If it's no trouble, I'd like a dozen handkerchiefs.

Shop Assistant   I've got some very nice ones. I'll show you right away.

Customer   Thank you!

Shop Assistant (*exits and comes back with various boxes*)
Look. You or whoever told you to buy them will be pleased
with them. And I'm pleased to be able to sell them to you.
The Greeks always put their faith in the final outcome.
They had very fast horses. I recommend you see *The
Centaurs of Numancia*, in cinemascope.

Customer   And are these other ones the same?

Shop Assistant   Oh, yes! (*He opens the other boxes.*) They've
got a slightly different pattern. Look at this one; it looks like
a meander. Nowadays there isn't a prophetic sense any
more. Delphic oracles keep silent. Eternally silent.

Customer   I'll have these.

Shop Assistant   How many would you like?

Customer   A dozen.

Shop Assistant   Fine. I'll just wrap them up for you.

Customer   Thank you!

Shop Assistant   Not at all! You'll be pleased with them.
My customers always are. (*Meanwhile he wraps them up.*) These
are quality handkerchiefs, they're incomparable. You or
whoever told you to buy them will be pleased with them.

Customer   Good.

Shop Assistant (*finishes wrapping them up*)   Athens was rich
in gold. When the sun rose, you could hear the first
songbirds. That was the life! Here you are.

Customer   Excuse me: have you got any towels?

Shop Assistant   Olympus in Greece had everything.

Customer   Thank you!

Shop Assistant   We're slaves to our customers. I'll show
you the towels in a second.

Customer   The best you've got, please.

Shop Assistant   Here you are! (*He shows him some towels.*) Look at them: excellent quality. They'll never wear out. Don't worry: they'll last you for ever. I know what I'm talking about. You or whoever told you to buy them . . .

Customer   How much are they?

Shop Assistant   A hundred pesetas each.

Customer   OK. I'd like a dozen.

Shop Assistant   Very good. A dozen, as well.

Customer   Thank you!

Shop Assistant   Thank you! (*He takes the towels and wraps them up.*) These towels are splendid.

Customer   And they're the best you've got, aren't they?

Shop Assistant   Yes sir, oh yes. In the Barcelona Olympus, we've always offered the best quality goods to our distinguished customers. Don't ever go to the shop next door. Before taking a decision, the Athenians always thought it over carefully. These handkerchiefs and towels will go well together in your home. Or it'll be a nice present, if it's a gift for someone . . .

Customer   Excuse me: I've changed my mind and I think for now I'll only buy the towels. Yes, yes, that's what I want. I'll come back soon.

Shop Assistant   Oh! As you wish. Fine: as you'll see, in this establishment, we're happy to serve our customers.

Customer   Let's change the handkerchiefs for the towels; yes.

Shop Assistant   As you wish. (*He gives him the wrapped-up towels.*) I'm your slave and I'm at your service.

Customer   Thank you! (*He takes the wrapped-up towels in a determined fashion, puts them under his arm and starts to exit.*)

Shop Assistant   Excuse me, sir . . . but . . .

Customer   Sorry? What do you want?

Shop Assistant (*nervously*)   Those towels cost three thousand two hundred pesetas.

Customer (*firmly*)   Yes, we'd already talked about that.

Shop Assistant   But I'm sorry . . . you haven't paid for them yet . . .

Customer   What do you mean I haven't paid for them! Didn't we agree they were in exchange for the handkerchiefs?

Shop Assistant   But you haven't paid for the handkerchiefs either . . .

Customer   Of course not! Am I taking them? . . . (*He exits in a determined fashion, leaving the* **Shop Assistant** *perplexed, scratching his head and looking at the audience.*)

Curtain.

The Audition
A Dialogue between an Aristocrat and an Actor

by

Rodolf Sirera

translated by

John London

'What would we have to do to satisfy such demanding judges? [. . .] Merely distance ourselves from all that is natural and fall prey to the wildest fantasies.'

Jean Racine, First Preface to *Britannicus*

For Joan Brossa

Premiere in Catalan
Broadcast on the television programme *Lletres Catalanes*, 18
October 1978, directed by Mercè Vilaret.

Premiere Production of the English translation
Gate Theatre, Notting Hill, London, 8 February 1988,
directed by Astrid Hilne; designed by Helen Tulley.

Gabriel de Beaumont   Carl Halling
Monsieur le Marquis de . . . Steven Dykes

Characters

Gabriel de Beaumont, actor
Monsieur le Marquis de . . .

The characters in this story are completely fictitious. The
period in which the play is set should emphasise the
impossibility of identifying them.

Paris, 1784. A private drawing-room in a rococo mansion. Furniture in keeping with the taste and style of the period. A section of the back wall forms a recess, framed by a large arch, the opening of which is covered by curtains. The remainder of the back wall is made up of a big latticed window, through which we can observe the inexorable advance of dusk. To the right and left, two closed doors. Seated in an armchair, **Gabriel de Beaumont** *is waiting to see* **Monsieur le Marquis de . . .** *A* **Servant**, *unsure on his feet, is lighting the candelabra with almost ceremonial slowness.*

Gabriel (*speaking loudly, after a long pause*)   The Marquis must surely have forgotten I'm here . . . (*The* **Servant** *does not reply. Silence.* **Gabriel** *insists again, in an indifferent tone.*) I presume you've reminded him that I've been waiting to see him . . . (*Short pause.*) for almost an hour . . . ? (*Confronted by the* **Servant**'s *refusal to speak, he pretends to be offended.*) Besides, it's not as if I'm the one who's particularly interested in this meeting . . . The Marquis himself . . . (*Stopping, unsure of himself. Then, with new-found confidence.*) Yes, he was the one . . . The Marquis wanted to meet me . . . Perhaps you didn't know? During the interval in yesterday's performance he sent me a message: 'I wish to speak for a few minutes with Monsieur Gabriel de Beaumont, actor . . .' However, my friend, an actor with my reputation is always busy . . . Take today, for example . . . I had to read several plays . . . (*We hear a clock strike six in the distance. With every stroke,* **Gabriel** *becomes more and more nervous.*) All right, that's enough! You're making me . . . nervous . . . You're like some kind of ghost, moving about for no reason! Do you think I give a damn whether you light twenty, or forty candles . . . ? As far as I'm concerned you can save yourself the bother. I'm leaving. (*Getting up.*) It's obvious that this is just a joke. The Marquis is clearly not going to see me today, and I still have a lot to do . . .

Servant (*in a neutral tone, continuing his work*)   The Marquis begs you to forgive him. He will be with you in a moment.

Gabriel (*sarcastically*)   God almighty! So you do have a tongue after all! For a moment, I thought you were a moving statue, not a human being!

Servant   The Marquis hopes that you will have an enjoyable stay in his house, and that you will have no cause for complaint . . .

Gabriel (*hesitating*)   I don't . . . especially . . . This room is very pleasant, but . . .

Servant   Allow me . . . (*He sets up a small table with drinks and glasses, taken from behind one of the side doors, which turns out to be the door to a large cupboard embedded in the wall.*) The Marquis has entrusted me to tell you that you can have everything you want at your disposal.

Gabriel   I don't want anything, thank you very much.

Servant (*as if he had not heard what* **Gabriel** *has just said*) I would in particular urge you to try this wine from Cyprus . . . It's a highly prized liqueur, with a rather exotic flavour . . . (*And he pours out a glass which* **Gabriel** *feels compelled to accept.*)

Gabriel   Very well . . . (*He drinks it all in one gulp, wanting to finish the conversation. He restrains himself from showing how unpleasant he finds the drink.*) But tell your master that I would be even more honoured if I could be graced by his presence as soon as possible. Is that understood?

Servant   I will tell the Marquis . . . (*He does not move an inch.*)

Gabriel   But if you stay here, I don't see how you can pass on my message! (*He becomes irritated again.*) Oh, for heaven's sake, do what I tell you!

Servant (*pouring him another glass*)   The Marquis does not need my help to know everything that goes on inside this mansion. (*Short pause.*) Might I persuade you to have another glass of this wine, Monsieur?

Gabriel (*drily*)   It's too sweet for my liking.

Servant (*in an impersonal tone*)   But the Marquis is most fond of it.

Gabriel (*finally giving in, and taking the glass*)   All right! But don't think you can shut me up with that kind of servility . . . (*He takes a sip and leaves the glass on the table.*) I've drunk it. Now what? (*His tone becomes harsher.*) What more do you all want with me? Why don't you go and carry out your duties?

Servant (*humbly*)   Monsieur . . .

Gabriel   You haven't stopped staring at me since you came in the room. Has the Marquis sent you to spy on me . . . ?

Servant (*taken aback*)   Oh no, Monsieur . . . ! (*Change of tone.*) It's just that . . . (*As if hesitating.*) On stage you look taller.

Gabriel (*surprised*)   Ah, that . . . (*Unconsciously becoming conceited.*) There's a simple reason for that. On stage, the audience is only given the points of reference we want to provide . . .

Servant (*softly*)   And your voice . . .

Gabriel (*amused, in spite of everything*)   It's stronger, more powerful . . . Is that what you mean? (*Didactically.*) That's only logical. Speaking with you, now, I don't have to worry about projecting my voice. There aren't any problems to do with distance or acoustics . . .

Servant (*stressing his interest*)   You mean that, when you act, you don't behave on stage the same as you do in real life . . . ?

Gabriel (*finally won over by the conversation*)   Of course not. That would be impossible . . . If I did, nobody would listen to me properly, and I wouldn't be able to convey the character's emotions . . .

Servant   Please forgive my insisting, but I'm fascinated by anything to do with the theatre. You said the characters' emotions. Did you really mean that, or were you perhaps referring to your own emotions, which, during the performance . . . ?

Gabriel (*interrupting him*)   No, no . . . They really are the character's emotions, but, in a way, they're mine as well. (*He sits down again, without stopping the flow of his speech.*) I mean that when you act, there comes a point at which you can't distinguish where fiction begins or ends . . .

Servant (*eagerly*)   Then you really have to feel what you express on stage . . . ?

Gabriel   Exactly: you express what you feel.

Servant   But, on the other hand, you yourself argued just now that you have to resort to a certain kind of speech . . . the correct projection of your voice . . . That is conventional. Besides, how can you really experience the emotions of Racine's characters, for example, when Racine, and all the other great writers of the past, express themselves through verse in a way which, as far as I can see, is hardly natural and, what's more, with words which aren't even in common use? . . .

Gabriel (*amused*)   You've turned out to be a proper philosopher, haven't you, just like Monsieur Diderot? (*Laughs.*) No, my friend, these disquisitions hardly suit your social class!

Servant (*undeterred*)   Excuse my saying so, Monsieur, but social classes are also a convention, like many other things.

Gabriel   Oh no; that's not true. Your Marquis, for example, exercises power . . . He has real, effective power . . . That power – and you probably realise this better than I do – is not exactly a social convention . . .

Servant   Yes, but you can rise from poverty to power, just as you can sink from power into poverty. A social status can be reversed . . .

Gabriel (*surprised*)   You must be one of the people who secretly subscribe to d'Alembert's Encyclopaedia! I've never heard a servant use such sophisticated language!

Servant   I don't see why you should be so surprised,
Monsieur . . . You have acquired a position for yourself in
society, but you're not an aristocrat . . . You've got where
you are through your effort alone, and that's an admirable
achievement . . .

Gabriel (*bitterly*)   A position in society . . . (*Restraining his
sudden unease.*)

Servant (*concerned, wishing to be of service*)   Monsieur . . .

Gabriel   That sweet wine can't have agreed with me. I
shouldn't have drunk it . . . It's always the same . . . (*Change
of tone.*) My position in society, you were saying? My position
in society is always rather precarious. It depends on my art,
and art depends on the tastes of a period . . . Anyway, my
background and my profession always rise up against me
like a brick wall or a kind of watchdog telling me: you're
entertained by kings and eat at their tables, but you'll never
reach their level. You'll always be an actor.

Servant (*deeply moved*)   An actor . . . The most despised and
yet most envied profession in the world. Everybody feels the
need to act once in a while . . . I mean, in real life; offstage
. . . (*After a short pause, as if deciding to make a great confession.*) I
myself . . .

Gabriel (*not realising the* **Servant**'s *growing excitement*)   I'm
not surprised. Servants' work always involves lying. If you're
a servant, you also have to act, and play a role . . .

Servant (*interrupting him, quickly*)   No, I didn't mean that
just now . . . It was really something much simpler. You see,
I've been acting for you. I've created a character . . . and
you, with all your experience, haven't been able to spot it.
So my acting has been a success. And that's because I've
behaved in a completely natural way.

Gabriel (*confused*)   What do you mean? I don't
understand . . .

Servant   It's simple: I'm not the Marquis's servant . . . (*Slowly, without looking at* **Gabriel**.) I am the Marquis . . . In person . . .

Gabriel (*after a pause. Unsure of himself, trying to show that he has not fallen for a joke which, moreover, he believes to be in rather dubious taste*)   Don't be ridiculous . . . That's impossible . . .

Servant (*continuing in the humble, discreet tone he has maintained from the beginning*)   Why is it impossible? How many times in your life have you seen the Marquis? In other words, how many times in your life have you seen me? Three or four . . . five at most; always some distance away, wearing his wig and his ceremonial robes . . . No . . . Think about it: it's very easy . . . A discreetly lit room, a different hairstyle, a plain jacket, and, above all, by carefully imitating a servant's way of talking and his mannerisms . . . That's all you need . . . (*He smiles.*) And in my innocence, I thought I wouldn't be able to keep up the fiction for a second, in front of a professional like you! Oh, did you really not realise? My conversation, what I said – not the way I said it – the . . . the depth of my arguments, my preoccupations . . . All that should have attracted your attention, all that gave me away . . . But no . . . You allowed yourself to be convinced by appearances . . . I was dressed as a servant, so I had to be a servant . . . But clothing is always a disguise.

Gabriel (*becoming more and more violent*)   With or without your disguise, you're not going to trick me, if that was what you had in mind! I know your sort only too well . . . ! (*Energetically.*) I'll call your master, and we'll all get an explanation for this.

Servant (*very calmly and softly*)   My friend, you shouldn't need any proof . . . You would act more wisely by believing what I tell you . . .

Gabriel (*now standing, having frantically pulled the rope for the* **Servant**'s *bell, as the* **Servant** *was speaking*)   Be quiet!

Servant (*after a long pause*)   You see? Nobody's going to answer. Do you still think I'm lying?

Gabriel (*stubbornly ringing the bell again and again; the echoes seem to disappear in distant rooms*)   I refuse to believe any of it. If nobody'll listen to me, I'll go myself! (*Goes to one of the side doors, but, in the heat of the moment, gets the wrong one, and opens the door to the cupboard from which the* **Servant** *had previously taken the drinks. He shuts it again angrily, and crosses the room to the other door.*)

Servant   That is a clothes cupboard (*He smiles.*), and the other door, which leads to the hall, is locked . . .

Gabriel (*after checking to see if he is telling the truth,* **Gabriel** *comes face to face with the* **Servant**)   Locked?

Servant   From the outside. Those were the orders I gave my servant.

Gabriel (*shouting*)   Locked from the outside? Have you gone out of your mind? Give me the key! (*Going towards him threateningly.*) Give me the key, or I'll *take* it from you! Do you hear?

Servant   Yes . . . But you're not so sure of yourself as you were a moment ago . . . You're beginning to hesitate . . .

Gabriel (*violently*)   The key!

Servant   Gabriel de Beaumont . . . (*The change in the* **Servant**'*s voice is so surprising that* **Gabriel** *is stopped in his tracks.*) If I am who I say I am, and you dare raise a finger against me . . . (*His tone is so harsh, that, even though he does not finish the sentence, it manages to create a long, intimidating silence in the room.*)

Gabriel (*recovering his calm, but now lacking his previous confidence*)   I'm not threatening you! You're keeping me here against my will!

Servant (*confidently*)   Unfortunately, there aren't any witnesses here to prove it. (*After a brief pause, tempering the* *severity in his voice.*) But no . . . I don't want to force you to do anything. I'm just asking you to listen to what I have to say. (*Crossing the stage to the door of the cupboard embedded in the wall.*) You're still not convinced. You won't believe I'm the Marquis, because I'm not dressed as a marquis. (*While he has been speaking, he has opened the cupboard door and taken out a wig which he substitutes for the one he was wearing, and an elegant dress coat, with which he replaces the* **Servant**'s *shabby jacket.*) All right: I'll do my best to satisfy you as quickly as I can. (*Once he is fully clothed, he closes the cupboard door, and turns towards* **Gabriel**, *who gapes at him in amazement.*) What's your answer now?

Gabriel (*stuttering*)   I . . . don't know . . . I'm confused . . .

Marquis* (*sitting down, he makes a conciliatory gesture to* **Gabriel**)   Please sit down, my friend . . . (**Gabriel** *sits down like an automaton.*) I wanted to speak to you, because I have a proposal to make . . . with reference to your profession . . . That explains the innocent game of disguises. I hope you'll forgive me, but I had to test you.

Gabriel (*following a pause. Very unsure of himself*)   Monsieur le Marquis . . . Is that what I should call you from now on? Please forgive me as well, but I'm still not sure. Are you . . . I mean, are you, Monsieur, really . . . the Marquis . . . ? Or is this another joke? But . . . I'm an idiot . . . The evidence you've just given me seems conclusive. Yes, you really are the Marquis. And I should have guessed it from the start . . . (*The social conventions gradually prevail, and* **Gabriel** *begins to react accordingly.*) You really have impressed me . . . And now I'm afraid I didn't behave as I should have, before. But, you've got to see my point of view . . . How could I ever know that . . . ? I mean . . . If I've in any way offended you . . .

Marquis (*in a friendly tone*)   Oh no . . . Everybody acts with other people according to their opinion of them . . . and according to the position they themselves think they have – or really do have – in society . . . Isn't that so? Now that you

*From now on, the **Servant** will be called the **Marquis**.

know I'm the Marquis, you've stopped speaking in that
condescending tone . . . that tone of superiority and self-
confidence with which you addressed the servant. Now
you're more polite with me and call me Monsieur le
Marquis. Right now, without realising it, you're also starting
to act . . .

Gabriel (*objecting hyperbolically*)   Monsieur! You mean to say
that . . . Oh! How could you doubt my sincerity?

Marquis   I don't doubt it, my friend! I was simply
pointing out a fact you probably weren't aware of yourself.
(*Short pause.*) In real life, as I was trying to explain before,
we all act . . . all the time . . . What's more, these daily
performances are vital for the survival of the social status
quo . . . Even for our own survival as individuals . . . Oh, if
Monsieur Rousseau's theories were taken seriously, we'd
live in a kind of hell on earth . . . ! (*This he says with a certain
morbid delight.*) The noble savage . . . (*Pause. He smiles.*)
No . . . Man at his most primitive is not exactly kind-
hearted . . . Of course, he's hardly hypocritical, I'll grant
you that . . . But that sort of sincerity, Gabriel . . . exposes
us for what we really are. And we're worse than the
cruellest beasts in the jungle . . . I'm speaking from my
own experience . . .

Gabriel   Even so, Monsieur le Marquis . . . in a century
as enlightened as ours, among our civilised contemporaries
. . . actions of extreme cruelty have been carried out . . . by
people who, given over to their most primitive instincts . . .

Marquis   Of course . . . But when I spoke of hell on
earth, I didn't do so with moral revulsion . . . or pious
condemnation . . . I was just objectively pointing out a fact
for which, I have to admit, I have a certain . . . shall we say
'aesthetic' admiration . . .

Gabriel (*surprised*)   Then, I don't understand you,
Monsieur le Marquis . . . How can such evil be . . .
beautiful?

Marquis   Oh, but . . . (*Rather disappointed.*) Don't you think it can? I'm surprised . . . Come now, when you play corrupt characters or murderers, don't you feel a certain envy deep down inside . . . ? I mean . . . when you shake off the skin of social conventions and established norms . . . and stop behaving as you're supposed to . . .

Gabriel (*very seriously*)   But that is fiction . . .

Marquis (*smiling again*)   Oh, yes . . . fiction . . . Of course . . . I was forgetting . . . (*Long pause. The* **Marquis** *gets up, goes to a piece of furniture, opens a drawer and takes out a book.*) I've invited you here because I want you to perform one of my plays.

Gabriel   One of your plays? I didn't know you were a writer, Monsieur le Marquis. (*He shows too much surprise and is thus unconvincing. The* **Marquis** *looks at him with curiosity.*)

Marquis   I've tried it out. (*Going up to* **Gabriel**.) Gabriel, I'd be very grateful if you could be the first person to perform it. I'll pay all the expenses. You'll be well rewarded if you agree to do it.

Gabriel   It's what I do for a living. (*Pause.*) Will you let me read it?

Marquis   Yes, but . . . (*Suddenly stops, without giving him the book.*) I must warn you now that my play is stylistically very different from the plays you act in. I can't guarantee you any great success.

Gabriel   I don't understand. Whenever an author writes a play he always wants it to be a success.

Marquis   I'm not really worried by what people think . . . (*Pause.*) No, Gabriel. My play is a piece of research. In it I want to prove – and, at the same time, demonstrate – my own theories: Monsieur Diderot states, quite categorically, that the best actors are the ones who are most distanced from their characters. Theatre is fiction, and, as such, the best way of recreating that fiction in an audience is, precisely, to imitate it, using one's mind. By your own account, you contradict yourself on this point. You told me that you are dominated by emotion when you act, that your own personality becomes tied up with the character you're playing; but you now admit that this identification is not total because, to achieve it, you use certain techniques: the projection of your voice, the correct movements, et cetera. As far as I'm concerned, I want to argue the opposite: that the best performances are those in which the actor *becomes* the character, lives his life as intensely as his own, and even loses all awareness of his own individuality. Drama should not be fiction, art or technique . . . Drama should be feeling, emotion . . . and, above all, the joy of transgressing established norms . . . We should experience all our suffering, all our anguish, all our most intimate desires and fears on stage . . . Gabriel . . . our reality . . . What we haven't the courage to admit or accept in everyday life, that's what I'm interested in . . . And I need men like you, Gabriel . . . brave and imaginative men, prepared to play the game to its limits . . . (**Gabriel**, *overcome by sudden tiredness, has fallen asleep. The* **Marquis**, *who has become progressively more excited in the course of his speech, notices* **Gabriel** *and stops. Softly, without the slightest hint of reproach, he goes up to* **Gabriel**, *and almost whispers in his ear.*) You're not listening . . .

Gabriel (*coming to with a jolt*)   Monsieur . . .

Marquis (*with a strange kind of affection which increases* **Gabriel**'*s unease*)   You fell asleep, Gabriel . . . You weren't listening to me . . .

Gabriel (*embarrassed, trying to justify himself*)   Monsieur le Marquis . . . I . . . I don't know what could have come over me . . . A moment ago, I suddenly felt extremely tired . . . But . . . no . . . it's nothing . . . I feel better already . . . Just the result of overwork . . . I'm tired, that's all . . . I'll get over it . . .

Marquis (*genuinely interested*)   Ah! You feel tired! (*Looking at his watch.*) Then we'll have to be quick . . . We haven't got much time left . . . (*As* **Gabriel** *tries to grab the glass of wine he left on the table.*) No! Don't drink that wine . . . now. It would make you sleepier, and I want you to be wide awake . . . (*He pours out a glass from another bottle, then hands it to* **Gabriel** *who anxiously drinks it. In a completely natural tone.*) Anyway, don't worry. As you say, you'll soon get over your tiredness and feel better. I *need* you feeling better. We have to carry out a test.

Gabriel   A test? (*Annoyed, since he feels his professional 'amour-propre' is being offended.*) You mean you don't trust my ability . . . my experience . . . ? Perhaps you think I'm some sort of amateur?

Marquis (*mellifluously*)   Oh, no, not at all . . . Don't misunderstand me. I want to test my play, not you.

Gabriel (*still annoyed*)   I don't understand you.

Marquis   I told you before that this play wasn't in any way like those which satisfy the . . . decadent tastes . . . of our times. I . . . (*Hesitating.*) I've read it to myself several times . . . alone, in my room . . . I've even read it out loud, but that isn't enough. I have to hear it . . . coming from your lips . . . brought to life by you . . .

He draws back the curtains of the great archway which forms a recess in the back wall, and a kind of apse is revealed with tiny grilled windows, but no door. The walls are made of plain stone. It looks like the 'theatrical' scenery for a medieval prison. In the centre of this stage, constituting the only piece of furniture, is a great stone seat, with back and arms, also in stone, rather like a royal throne.

Look . . . I've prepared the ideal setting for you . . .

Gabriel   But I . . . I can't . . . I can't act for you like this . . . without knowing the play . . . not having rehearsed it . . . I'd have to read it first, and try and understand the action and the characters . . . (*Since the* **Marquis** *does not answer him because he is lighting the candles for the stage,* **Gabriel**, *now becoming progressively more nervous, goes up to the proscenium of the* *little theatre.*) At least tell me what it's about . . . the subject, the setting, the plot . . . something . . .

Marquis (*continuing what he is doing*)   Do you really think that is so important . . . ? (*Stops what he is doing, turns round and faces* **Gabriel**. *In a more gentle voice.*) Oh, all right . . . It's a free adaptation of the life of Socrates, from Xenophon's Apology. But, how can I put it . . . ? I'm not really interested in the plot itself . . . I could have written the play about any other character or setting that happened to come to mind . . .

Gabriel   But Socrates . . .

Marquis (*stepping off the stage*)   Socrates is just a pretext, Gabriel. It's not really about his life . . . It's about his death. The process of his death, *that* is what I wanted to examine.

Gabriel (*rather sceptically*)   His death? Then, the psychology . . . the historical facts we all know . . .

Marquis (*self-satisfied*)   There you have it: we all know them. Since we all know them, it's better to ignore them. (*He smiles.*) Anyway, all that psychology . . . bah! it's just an excuse for philosophising . . . No . . . The only thing we don't know about Socrates – and so many other characters – is, precisely, their death. Not the fact they died, that's obvious . . . or even the way they died, and not the cause of their death . . . But their death . . . I repeat, the process of their death . . . Dying with them . . . Not seeing how they die, but feeling the intensity of their death . . . our own death . . .

Gabriel (*impressed*)   Feeling, again . . .

Marquis   Yes, feeling! Feeling, Gabriel! Feeling without rhetoric . . . Somehow taking part in their agony; making our bodies experience, our minds perceive, step by step, stage by stage, the inescapable advance towards self-destruction . . .

Gabriel   You mean, lead the condemned man to the gallows?

Marquis (*quickly*)   But I don't just mean that . . . If only
we could, through some kind of imitative magic, penetrate
and live their inner life while still being ourselves . . . then,
what sublime delight, what pleasure for the mind! And just
imagine how that pleasure would be conveyed, and spread
to every part of our poor bodies! What pleasure, Gabriel, in
this, our dreary age of rationalism! (*He laughs.*) But, as you
can see . . . I go on and on . . . and lose myself in words . . .
(*Looks at his watch again.*) I was enjoying emotions which I
haven't yet even managed to stir up in you . . . (*Pause. Then,
with apparent indifference.*) You still haven't said if you'll agree
to play my game . . .

Gabriel (*finally giving in to his host's whims, somewhat wearily*)   I
don't understand you, Monsieur, but if it'll make you happy,
I'll gladly perform an extract from your play. Tell me what
you want me to do. (*As he climbs up on to the stage.*) However, I
must warn you that, without a rehearsal, I won't be able to
do anything very impressive first time round; but, since you
insist . . .

Marquis   Oh, yes, I do, Gabriel . . . I do . . . (*He quickly
climbs up on to the stage as well and inspects everything closely.*) Wait
a minute . . . (*Satisfied, having finished checking everything.*) Yes . . .
yes, everything is in place . . . (*Steps down from the stage, picks up
the book, opens it at the corresponding page and, going up to the
proscenium, hands the book to* **Gabriel**.) I'm particularly
interested in this scene . . .

Gabriel (*from the stage, once he has glanced at the open page*)
The death scene . . .

Marquis   Exactly.

Gabriel   But . . . the other characters . . .

Marquis   We can do without them . . .

Gabriel   All right. (*Goes towards the stone throne.*)

Marquis   Don't move from the throne. You no longer
have any strength left.

Gabriel (*sitting down*)   In a sitting position for the whole scene?

Marquis   Yes.

Gabriel   That'll mean I won't be able to strike certain poses . . . for example, tragic poses . . .

Marquis   Forget about that. We'll assume you're dying.

Gabriel   I see. (*Following a pause.*) But . . .

Marquis (*impatiently*)   Why won't you begin?

Gabriel   I was wondering . . .

Marquis   There's no time for that now. (*Correcting his tone.*) Oh! (*Returning to a polite tone.*) What is it?

Gabriel   If you're so obsessed with . . . reality . . . (*With a hidden note of sarcasm.*) aren't you surprised that I'm not wearing Greek robes?

Marquis (*without thinking*)   No. You've got to . . . (*Suddenly stopping, as if taken aback by what he has just said.*) No, for the time being, no . . . (*Changes to an artificially light tone.*) I'll explain it all to you later. You wouldn't understand now . . . (*He smiles.*) or you wouldn't believe me.

Gabriel (*who obviously does not understand what the* **Marquis** *means*)   Ah . . . (*Long pause. Hesitantly.*) Then . . . dressed as I am . . . ?

Marquis (*firmly*)   Yes. It's essential for you to do it dressed as you are.

Gabriel   All right. You're the one who's directing the performance.

Marquis (*softly*)   Yes, Gabriel, I am, to all intents and purposes, the director.

Gabriel   Fine. Will you give me just a few seconds to get into the scene?

Marquis   Take your time.

Gabriel   Thank you. (*He reads the open page quickly, but closely. Long silence. He suddenly begins to proclaim in a rather affected manner.*) Tell me, friends . . . Tell me, you who are by me in this fatal hour . . . what is expected of me . . . what pose does history require me to strike . . . in my death . . . ? A heroic pose, with an expression of eternal rest on my face . . . An example to be followed . . . But history knows nothing about death . . . about the deaths of individuals . . . History despises isolated cases. It generalises. It has no desire to know about symptoms, vital processes . . . It is only interested in the results. And what about me? What am I in all this machinery? Nothing more than a myth. And myths cannot cry out. (*Pause. The* **Marquis** *unconsciously begins to shake his head gently in disagreement, but* **Gabriel**, *gradually becoming more and more involved in the scene, does not notice.*) But men are the ones who die . . . And men die painfully, in convulsions, crying out for mercy . . . they die pathetically . . . soiling their bedclothes with excrement and the blood of their vomit . . . and they're scared . . . they're scared . . . terrified . . . not by a religious fear of what awaits them . . . no . . . by a nameless fear . . . the physical fear of the physical death everyone suffers . . . because death is consecration, it's the great ceremony of fear . . . Can't you understand that?

Marquis (*suddenly, in a tone of indifference*)   No.

Gabriel (*surprised, interrupts his performance. Not knowing what to say, hesitating*)   Pardon?

Marquis   All I said was no; I can't. Or, at least, I can't understand that from your performance.

Gabriel (*rising from the throne, restraining his anger. Slowly*) Does that mean you don't like my acting?

Marquis   What I mean is that your style of acting doesn't manage to convey what's happening to the character. (*Convinced of what he is saying.*) How can I understand, when I can't feel what you're supposed to be feeling?

Gabriel (*icily*)   Your opinion of my artistic abilities, Monsieur le Marquis, seems rather personal, and is, in practice, contradicted by the overwhelming majority of Parisian audiences. And, when I say audiences, I'm obviously also referring to intelligent people . . . *people as intelligent and as learned as yourself.*

Marquis (*in a conciliatory tone*)   Gabriel, please . . . Listen . . .

Gabriel (*who can no longer contain his anger, goes up to the edge of the small stage*)   In other words, you invited me to your home and made me act out this absurd farce just so you could make fun of me. Well, I'm sorry, but I won't play your game any more. I don't like being insulted. And, as far as I'm concerned, questioning my artistic talent would be like questioning your nobility.

Marquis (*without raising his voice*)   You're not making any effort to try and understand. My play is totally different from all other plays . . .

Gabriel (*scornfully*)   I've realised that. But I don't see how the two things are connected.

Marquis   It's obvious: a different literary style requires a completely new style of acting.

Gabriel (*in a tone of superiority*)   Oh, of course . . . ! You're not content with making your debut as a dramatist. You also feel obliged to give me lessons about my profession.

Marquis (*patiently*)   All I mean is you can't adequately perform what you haven't ever experienced . . . What you haven't experienced directly and personally. Because you've never gone through the agony of real death . . .

Gabriel (*whose sarcasm is barely restrained*)   If I'd gone through the agony of real death, I would have died, and then I wouldn't be able to perform the part. (*Surprised by his own reasoning.*) Oh, you'll have me talking real rubbish in a minute! (*Trying to explain what he means.*) According to your argument, every time an actor performed the death of a character . . . (*Stopping. Not knowing whether he should become yet angrier or burst out laughing.*) But, for heaven's sake! Do you think I'm an idiot? Characters who die on stage every night come back to life after the performance is over. And that's how plays are repeated, day after day.

Marquis (*as if thinking out loud*)   But they're never exactly the same in every performance . . . There are always . . . small differences . . .

Gabriel   Exactly. Small differences, that's all.

Marquis (*becoming progressively more excited as he speaks*)   But I want to make my play a unique example! Just as my paintings are unique examples . . . my furniture . . . my clothes . . . (*He walks round the room excitedly.*) and my books . . . (*He points to some books, standing upright between two classical statues, on a piece of furniture.*) My books as well . . . Unique editions, of my favourite texts, made to my specifications . . .

Gabriel (*without understanding*)   But in the theatre, that's impossible. With the text of a play, maybe . . . But in the performance of it . . .

Marquis (*quickly*)   In the performance as well, Gabriel . . . ! The performance is precisely what I'm interested in!

Gabriel   And where are you going to keep it, then? (*Amused.*) You can't frame a theatrical performance, like a picture, or put it on a shelf . . .

Marquis   I want to keep it here . . . (*Pointing to his head.*) In my memory . . .

Gabriel (*shrugging his shoulders*)   If this is just one of your whims . . .

Marquis (*solemnly*)   It's not a whim, it's a need.

Gabriel (*following a pause, in a tone of contrived indifference;* **Gabriel** *is about to step off the stage*)   All right . . . Sorry. It seems I'm not good enough for you. You'll have to look for another actor who can attain the level of realism you require. Though, if you don't mind my saying so, I very much doubt you'll find one. In one way or another, we are all products of the same school.

Marquis   But I don't want anybody else; I need you!

Gabriel (*confused*)   But you said that . . .

Marquis (*annoyed*)   You won't let me finish . . . You won't let me finish, and we've both almost forgotten that time is running out . . . (*As if speaking to himself.*) Time is running out . . . And that could be very dangerous . . .

Gabriel   Dangerous? Why . . . ? I don't understand.

Marquis   Oh, how can you understand, when every time I try and go into details, you make me lose my train of thought, with your academic disquisitions . . . which are now completely off the point? (**Gabriel** *suddenly seems unable to keep his balance. He raises his hands to his head and stifles a groan. The* **Marquis** *looks at him anxiously.*) What's wrong? Are you all right?

Gabriel   My head's turning . . . I feel dizzy . . . It's strange . . . It's as if my legs won't support me . . . If you'll allow me to . . . sit down . . . I need to sit down for a bit . . . (*He drowsily stumbles towards the throne, and sits down. The* **Marquis** *does not move or give the slightest indication of wanting to help him.*) Forgive me . . . but I find it very difficult . . . to concentrate . . . You'll have to forgive me . . . I can't . . . I can't follow your arguments . . . Honestly . . . I can't remember . . . I don't know what you were talking about . . . I've forgotten . . . And, really . . . now . . . I don't even know the reason why . . . I'm . . . suddenly . . . so tired . . .

Marquis (*calmly, after a short pause*)   The reason? The reason is very simple, Gabriel . . . The reason is a combination of that Cypriot wine . . . and the clock . . .

Gabriel   The . . . wine?

Marquis (*becoming impatient*)   Oh! Do I have to spell it out to you in black and white, as if you were some kind of schoolboy? I wanted to test you, Gabriel! You've been part of my experiment!

Gabriel (*now beginning to react and show his fear*)   An . . . artistic experiment? Is that what you mean?

Marquis   No, of course not! An experiment in physiology . . . applied to an actor's technique.

Gabriel   Physiology . . . (*Suddenly realising everything: he is terrified, but does not have the strength to stand up.*) The wine! That's what it is . . . ! Oh, no! No! Oh, God, no! How could you do that!

Marquis (*energetically*)   I had to know!

Gabriel (*panic-stricken; shouting*)   You had to know? There's only one thing anybody has to know; and that's that you're a murderer!

Marquis (*with dignity*)   I'm not a murderer! I'm a scientist! The realm of aesthetics is artificial, and I can't bear artificiality. The only thing I'm interested in is the study of human behaviour! Human beings are real, living things, and the study of them gives me greater pleasure than all your plays and symphonies put together!

Gabriel   You're mad! You're inhuman!

Marquis (*triumphant*)   You see? Your attitude towards me is changing! *Now* . . . *Now* you're really afraid! Now you're really afraid, and your fear isn't simulated! You know you're going to die . . . That you've only got a few minutes left to live . . . Oh! This is the ideal moment to carry out my experiment! You're going to die just like my character! Fiction retreats, defeated by reality! There aren't two views of the world any more! Only one view, one unique view, the truth! The truth above all emotions and social conventions . . . ! The truth, Gabriel! The truth is as precious as life itself!

Gabriel (*who has struggled to reach a standing position, takes a few steps forward towards the footlights. Having lost all self-control, in a* *hoarse voice*)   If I must die, I'll kill you as well! I'll use all the strength I have left to get my revenge!

Marquis (*stands firm; authoritatively*)   Wait a minute, Gabriel! Stop! Let me propose . . . a pact . . .

Gabriel (*hesitant, but still stepping forward*)   There's no time left . . . There's no time left for that . . .

Marquis   Yes there is. (*Looking at his watch.*) Exactly eight minutes.

Gabriel (*finally stopping, without stepping off the stage*)   What?

Marquis   The drug is gradually taking over your body . . . your movements . . . but you'll be able to think clearly for a minute or two more . . . (*Short pause. Energetically.*) You want to save your own life, don't you? All right. Whether or not you do will depend on your own intelligence. (*Takes a small bottle out of his pocket, and shows it to* **Gabriel**.) You see this little bottle? It's the antidote.

Gabriel (*threatening again*)   Give it to me! I'll kill you if you don't!

Marquis (*unmoved*)   If you dare step off that stage, I'll smash the bottle on the floor.

Gabriel (*after a long period of silence, his will is broken and he drops down, defeated, sobbing, overcome by an attack of hysteria*) Oh, no! No . . . ! I . . . I don't want to die . . . I didn't mean what I said before . . . ! I don't want to die . . . !

Marquis (*dispassionately, as if talking about a petty commercial transaction*)   Stop crying, and listen. Will you accept my conditions? (**Gabriel**, *holding back his tears, nods humbly, without rising from his position on the floor.*) All right: you're going to give another performance.

Gabriel (*beginning to cry again, frightened*)   Act . . . Oh, no! . . . I . . . couldn't . . .

Marquis (*unpitying*)   You're going to have to.

Gabriel   Even if I did . . . my performance would be . . . ah . . . would be . . . (*Holding back his tears.*) disastrous . . .

Marquis   It's going to have to be your best performance yet, Gabriel. If I don't like it . . . If I don't like it . . . I won't give you the antidote.

Gabriel (*glimpsing in the **Marquis**'s words a last glimmer of hope for the condemned man*)   Do you swear? I mean, do you swear . . . Do you swear that if I manage to . . . ?

Marquis (*interrupting him*)   I give you my word of honour. (*Brief pause. Looking at his watch again.*) You have six minutes left, Gabriel. A six-minute performance, in exchange for your life. And, if you do save your own life, I can assure you that you'll be paid more than you've earned in the course of your career. But don't waste time now. Make an effort to concentrate and be ready to begin at once. (*Opens the drawer of the little table and takes out a small sand-glass which he places on the table, beside the bottle containing the antidote.*) When all the sand has dropped into the lower half of the sand-glass, the performance will end, and you will find out if you have passed the test. (*Sits down in an armchair, next to the table on which he has placed the sand-glass and the bottle.*) I'm ready when you are.

*After a pause, **Gabriel** drags himself up off the ground, and stumbles back to the throne. He sits down, picks up the book, and examines the open page with an impenetrable expression. Silence. **Gabriel** eventually nods to the **Marquis**, but does not look him in the face. The **Marquis** solemnly says:*

Marquis   The performance is now beginning.

*Then, the **Marquis**, slowly and with almost ceremonial care, turns the sand-glass upside down so that the sand starts to fall. **Gabriel**, as if jerked into action by an invisible spring, simultaneously begins his performance.*

Gabriel, *in spite of his physical state, is clearly seen to be making a great effort of willpower to excel. He is tense, concentrating on his role and trying to vary each part of the speech, each word, and to imbue* *every movement of his arms and head with meaning; even his slightest, most insignificant gestures are moved by a primitive desire to transcend his present wretchedness as an actor, and raise it to the category of a great sacrificial rite, offered up to the implacable categories of a supreme beauty, free from affectation. Acting against himself, contrary to his own intuition, contrary to his convictions and his artistic experience,* **Gabriel** *devotes body and soul to the search for vibrant intonations which are, at the same time, full of humility, and completely removed from the rhetorical formulations he used in his first reading of the extract. His acting thereby becomes so natural, so sincere, that his first performance of the text seems artificial by comparison. He speaks very slowly, alert even during the pauses; he is carried along by his own vital rhythm, and is brilliantly fused with his character. In his eagerness, the* **Marquis** *holds his breath and stares at the actor's face. Thick beads of sweat begin to appear on the foreheads of both men. Every pause, every new word gathers on the walls and the furniture, which echo the mysterious rhythms and forebodings of death and hope.*

Gabriel   Tell me, friends . . . Tell me, you who are by me in this fatal hour . . . what is expected of me . . . what pose does history require me to strike . . . in my death . . . ? A heroic pose, with an expression of eternal rest on my face . . . An example to be followed . . . But history knows nothing about death . . . about the deaths of individuals . . . History despises isolated cases. It generalises. It has no desire to know about symptoms, vital processes . . . It is only interested in the results. And what about me? What am I in all this machinery? Nothing more than a myth. And myths cannot cry out. But men are the ones who die . . . And men die painfully, in convulsions, crying out for mercy . . . they die pathetically . . . soiling their bedclothes with excrement and the blood of their vomit . . . and they're scared . . . they're scared . . . terrified . . . not by a religious fear of what awaits them . . . no . . . by a nameless fear . . . the physical fear of the physical death everyone suffers . . . because death is consecration, it's the great ceremony of fear . . . Can't you understand that?

Gabriel *stops when he reaches this point. It is exactly the same point at which he was interrupted by the* **Marquis** *in the first reading.* **Gabriel** *is in a state of panic because he knows that the fatal answer will soon be given; he cannot go on. The consequences of the great effort he has made to keep his self-control and act without showing his real state start to become more and more apparent.*

Marquis (*after a long period of silence, faced by* **Gabriel**'s *questioning, anguished expression, and realising that the actor's resistance has reached its breaking point*)   There's no need for you to go on. (*Pause.* **Gabriel** *does not dare say anything. He is afraid to ask. The* **Marquis** *prolongs the tension of the situation by speaking very slowly.*) All of the sand hasn't yet dropped . . . (*He picks up the sand-glass and leaves it in a horizontal position on the table.*) But that will do.

He stands up, takes the bottle containing the antidote, and walks very slowly to the table with the drinks service. The position of his body makes it impossible to see exactly what he is doing. He prepares a glass of wine and, holding it, he slowly walks up to the stage. **Gabriel** *watches the* **Marquis**'s *every movement with a mixture of eagerness and fear. The silence is unbearable. The* **Marquis** *climbs on to the stage. He goes up to* **Gabriel** *and gives him the glass.* **Gabriel** *does not move or say anything. He stretches out his arm and takes the glass with a trembling hand. He lifts the glass to his lips. He drinks from it. He sighs deeply and shuts his eyes. The* **Marquis** *takes the glass from him and moves back towards the footlights.* **Gabriel**'s *body begins to shake rhythmically. He is crying. His crying is stifled and quiet, like that of a child. The* **Marquis** *steps off the stage and looks at* **Gabriel** *affectionately.*

Marquis   Don't cry. It's hardly dignified for a man like you.

Gabriel (*without looking at the* **Marquis**, *unable to hold back his tears*)   I . . . can't . . . help it . . . I'm crying for joy . . .

Marquis (*softly*)   Then I admire your bravery. (*Goes to the side of the stage from which he drew back the curtains, and presses an ornamental moulding in the wall. A large grid of bars silently starts to descend from the ceiling; in just a few seconds it reaches the floor,*

thereby completely shutting off the opening to the small stage.) Yes . . .
You're very brave, Gabriel. You're braver than I thought.
Because you played against me . . . because you risked
playing against me, Gabriel, and you've lost the game . . .
and you've ended up by cheerfully accepting defeat.

Gabriel (*slowly lifting up his head and seeing the bars. Does not
move. Destroyed, overcome by nervous tension, now unable to raise his
voice*)   I've . . . lost . . . ! You . . . you said that . . . You gave
me . . . your word of honour . . .

Marquis (*returning to his armchair. Before sitting down, he faces*
Gabriel *and says*)   And I'm keeping it. I never said I liked
your performance.

Gabriel   But you . . . Oh no . . . ! You've just given me
. . . the antidote . . .

Marquis (*takes the small bottle out of his pocket, in the same state
that it was before, and shows it to* **Gabriel**. *Calmly*)   I haven't
given you any antidote, Gabriel. In fact, I've just poisoned
you.

Gabriel (*who can no longer react. In a weak voice*)   But . . . the
wine . . .

Marquis   I never said that wine – the first one you drank
when you came here – was poisoned. No . . . Think about it
. . . That was what you assumed, because of certain
symptoms . . . (*Sits down in his armchair.*) It was only a light
drug. A harmless drug to make you feel sleepy and slow
down your bodily reactions. (*Smiles.*) I had to protect myself
against the possibility of any violence on your part . . . (*Brief
pause. Showing him the bottle again.*) If you'd taken the antidote,
all of the symptoms I described would have disappeared in a
few minutes. That is physiology, Gabriel. You alone, your
imagination created all that visceral fiction of agony. The
only real poison, the only lethal poison, for which I swear,
there is no known antidote, is the one you've just drunk.
(*Smiles again. Softly.*) You see? In no way have I deceived you.
(*Looking at his watch.*) I told you before that you had a few

minutes left to live, and that was also true. The difference lies in the fact that you thought you had already swallowed the poison, and the last few minutes were all you had left before its full effect would be felt. But I tried to explain that what would be decided then, at the end of the test, was simply, whether you lived . . . or died. From the moment you drank the poison, you were dead, Gabriel. (*Puts his pocket watch away.*) Your time is up, and you can't make any more decisions about your life or your actions. Death is making you its slave. It's locked you in its prison . . . and made sure the doors are firmly shut.

Gabriel (*articulating with difficulty*)   But . . . why . . . the . . . bars . . . ?

Marquis   Because, from now on, the course of your agony starts to become dangerous. (*Gets up, and goes over to the stage.*) And I want to be able to contemplate it at my leisure, without having to worry about my safety.

Gabriel (*desperately snatching at a last, futile hope*) 'Contemplate' the death of a human being . . . No . . . That's impossible . . . You . . . you couldn't do that . . . You've played another trick on me . . . It's a game . . . another lie . . . (*He tries to laugh, his face contorted in a grotesque grimace.*) You want to frighten me, that's all . . . You love making me suffer . . . don't you? (*His voice ends up betraying what he really feels. He is crying; all his 'élan' has disappeared; choking, exhausted.*) Please tell me . . . Tell me it's not true . . . Tell me I'm dreaming . . .

Marquis (*unmoved*)   No, Gabriel . . . you're not dreaming . . . Unfortunately for you, and fortunately for me. I said I wanted you to give a unique performance. But perhaps I didn't use the right words. You're not going to act for me. You'll be playing for real. Now do you understand? The only way of adequately acting out your own death – you said so before, but you were only joking – is, precisely . . . : when you actually die . . .

Gabriel   Before . . . I was . . . acting . . . acting out my fear . . . I was scared, I . . . thought I was dying . . .

Marquis   Oh, yes, before . . . Before you were scared, yes . . . there's no doubt about that. You were very scared, but that wasn't enough for me. You still had a glimmer of hope left. You were playing against me. You wanted to win. And, so, because you were playing, you still didn't think you had definitely lost. You weren't completely beaten as you are now. (*He laughs.*) Ah, Gabriel . . . ! You've kept your acting instinct till the finale. Right up until the end you've pretended to be a character. (**Gabriel** *sighs deeply and his head falls lifelessly down on to his chest.*) What's wrong? Poor Gabriel, you've fallen asleep again . . . You've fallen asleep, because you've no other way of escaping . . . Because you can't bear to see your life slipping helplessly through your fingers, as each minute goes by . . . each breath . . . each heartbeat . . . each pause . . . (*Changes to an impersonal tone.*) But no. It doesn't matter. In a few moments you'll wake up again. The effects of the first drug will have worn off, and you'll be full of energy and thinking clearly. And the poison, the real poison, will gradually begin to act on your body . . . very slowly . . . and painfully . . . for several hours . . . But let's not rush things, Gabriel. Let's respect the conventions and the formality of our art . . . We'll go and sit down. (*Sits down again in the armchair.*) And now, Gabriel, if you don't mind, I will stop talking. The curtain has just risen. A rather delicate piece of music is being played on violins which are concealed from view. The stage is lit by scores of candles, and the leading actor, dressed for the ceremony, is getting ready to make a dramatic entrance . . . Ah, this moment of expectation is sublime . . . Just think of the tension which can be concentrated in these few seconds before the first speech . . . But let's stop talking now . . . Will members of the audience kindly remain in their seats? . . . Let's respect all the ritual and be quiet. Not a word. Tonight is the opening night and the performance is about to begin . . . right now. (*Very slowly, all the lights go out until darkness covers the stage.*)

Desire

by

Josep Maria Benet i Jornet

translated by

Sharon G. Feldman

To Domènec Reixach and Sergi Belbel,
without whom this play would not
have come to fruition

Premiere in Catalan
Teatre Romea, Barcelona, 8 February 1991, directed by
Sergi Belbel.

Premiere of the English translation
Rehearsed reading in The Studio, Royal Exchange Theatre,
Manchester, 11 November 1999, directed by Suzanne Bell
(as part of the 'Made in Spain' series).

The Husband	Simon Coury
She	Julia Stubbs
The Man	David Crellin
The Woman	Martine Brown

Characters

The Husband
She
The Man
The Woman

I

The light comes up. Elements which identify a single-family residence, not too large, situated far from the city. There is a table and there could be a window through which enters the light of this sunless day. **She** *has a bag open and removes several objects from it, a mixture of tools necessary for the upkeep of the home.* **The Husband** *enters; he carries a toolbox and a partially constructed wooden contraption.*

The Husband   Oh.

She   What?

The Husband   You'll probably need the table.

She   I do need it.

The Husband   Damn, it's cold!

He sits down on the floor, opens the box. He takes out a hammer, pliers, nails, a chisel . . .

She   What are you going to do here, now?

The Husband   You need the table.

She   You'll dirty the floor and then, you, you won't sweep up. Go and play outside.

The Husband   Play . . .

She   Well, if it's not any fun, stop it.

The Husband   I want to finish today.

She   We shouldn't have come.

The Husband *has begun to work, trimming the wood with the chisel, fitting together pieces, trying holes, nailing nails . . .*

The Husband   The girls picked a fine day.

She   All in all, we picked a fine day.

The Husband   They could catch cold hiking in the mountains. Here we've got good heating.

She   When the house does finally heat up it'll be time for us to leave.

The Husband   It'll heat up in an hour, and we're leaving tomorrow evening.

She   Tomorrow afternoon.

The telephone rings.

The Husband   We'll decide later. (*He picks up the receiver, since* **She** *has not moved.*) Hello. Yes, just a minute. (*To her.*) For you.

She *stops what she was doing and goes to take the receiver from* **The Husband**'s *hands.*

She   Hello. Hello. (*Annoyed.*) Hello! (*To* **The Husband**.) Did they ask for me?

The Husband   Yes.

She   No one is saying anything. Hello! (*Waits a moment and hangs up.*)

The Husband   A problem with the connection.

She   Who could it be?

The Husband   I don't know. A woman.

She   Which one?

The Husband   I didn't recognise her voice. She'll call again.

The telephone goes click.

She   Now they've hung up.

The Husband   She'll call again.

She   And on top of everything, it's as though we were completely cut off from the rest of the world.

The Husband (*calmly*)   You liked it. You liked the place and you liked the house. With the central heating installed and the phone connected.

She   Hello, hello, but no one answers.

The Husband   It's a good house. At least on Saturdays and Sundays, not having to put up with the noise in the city.

She   Next time we should bring more blankets.

The Husband   And in summer, you'll see.

She   At least lay some newspaper down and put your inventions on top of it. You'll scratch the floor.

The Husband   Give it to me.

She *hands him some of the crumpled paper from which she has been unpacking objects.*

She   Here. (**The Husband** *will open up the paper, place it on the floor and put all his tools on it.*) I need to do some shopping.

The Husband   Get me some cigarettes.

She   If I remember. Rice, olive oil, salt, vinegar, clothes-pegs, a tin-opener . . . I should probably write it all down.

The Husband   Write down the cigarettes.

She   She hasn't called back. Well, you'll need to tell the phone company.

The Husband   What?

She   Whoever phoned hasn't called back.

The Husband   Are you expecting a call?

She   Last week the same thing, exactly the same.

The Husband   In the city, the lines don't work so well either.

She   I'm off to the superstore.

The Husband   They may call while you're gone.

She   Half an hour by car. If only there was a shop nearby . . .

The Husband   There will be. And the cafeteria is always there for emergencies.

She   We should have bought a house in a village; they're not so isolated.

The Husband   We're not so isolated; there aren't a lot of people but we're not so isolated.

She   Shopping, and to think that I came here to rest. Half an hour there and half an hour back.

The Husband   I'll go, later.

She   I'm going, right now.

The Husband   What's the matter? (*He gets up. He moves closer.*) If something's wrong, tell me what it is.

She   Nothing is wrong.

The Husband   The house is fine. The thing is you have to make it your own.

She (*with a mocking laugh*)   What a thing to say! Your snoring won't let me sleep tonight.

The Husband   Right, the problem is my snoring.

She   The problem is there isn't any problem. The problem, you yourself said so, the problem is I don't know what the girls are doing out on a hike in this weather.

The Husband   I thought I was the one who was worried about the girls.

She   And this place is too isolated. (*Pause.*) It didn't seem as if it had broken down, the phone I mean.

The Husband   When?

She   Now, I'm talking about now. They asked for me, right? And I got to the phone and that was it. It didn't seem as if it had broken down.

The Husband   There must have been some problem, they couldn't talk to you.

She   Maybe they didn't want to talk to me.

The Husband   She asked for you.

She   Right.

The Husband   Well?

She   You never see anyone on this road, until you get to the main road, since there are so few of us on the estate.

The Husband   The day will come when you'll miss it.

She   I'll say it, and you'll probably say it's my imagination.

The Husband   I'll say what about what?

She   But it's true, I'm not mad.

The Husband   Why should you be mad.

She   What do you mean, that you're the one who's mad and it's my fault?

The Husband   That's right, go ahead and confuse everything . . .

She   Poor thing. Would you like a beer? I think I'll have a beer before I go.

She *takes one from some place.* **She** *has already put away all the objects which were in the bag and on the table only the papers in which they were wrapped remain, which, between gulps of beer –* **She** *drinks from the bottle –* **She** *will go about folding.*

The Husband   I don't want any beer.

She   Two or three beers a day won't do any harm.

The Husband   And maybe you'll be in a good mood again. That is if you don't start remembering that the drink is making you lose your figure.

She   Well, it's not my imagination, I get the feeling that . . . I didn't say anything to you about it because it was as if I'd already heard your answer. The same one you'll give when I've told you about it.

The Husband   What do you want to tell me about?

She   How many times have I gone to the superstore, from here, by myself?

The Husband   I haven't counted.

She   Three times. In the two months that we've begun to settle in, three times.

The Husband   And I've only gone once. I'm sorry.

She   Shut up. The first time, not a thing.

The Husband   The first time you went to the superstore.

She   Yes, not a thing. I mean, normal. On the road, no one passed by; normal. I left, I took the main road to the store, I loaded up the car, turned back, and nothing. Not a soul on the road. By the way, yes, I did stop at the cafeteria, I decided to stop and have a look round. And have a beer, of course. I don't see how it could be of any use to us. It's a dreadful place. It won't be of any use to us.

The Husband   It's better to have it there than not have it at all.

She   Anyway, that day, nothing. But it was the second time. I thought of it because of what happened with the phone. The second time, on the road, I saw a parked car. And outside, standing there in the middle, a man was signalling for me to stop.

The Husband   A breakdown?

She   I suppose so. I didn't stop.

The Husband   Right.

She   I didn't want to be bothered.

The Husband   Of course.

She   I wasn't happy about doing it. It was just so deserted that I couldn't stop.

The Husband   The man must have cursed you. Did he look dangerous?

She   Dangerous? He looked pathetic.

The Husband   Have you finished folding the papers?

She   I'm finishing up now.

The Husband   I'll be using the table. If you make a list, remember the cigarettes.

She   Are you listening to me or not?

The Husband   Haven't I been listening to you?

She   I haven't finished yet. There's still the third time, that was the second.

The Husband   It's just that I don't know what it is you're telling me.

She   Because you won't let me finish. You're not interested in what I'm saying.

The Husband   Let's see if we're lucky and the weather changes tomorrow.

She   What?

The Husband   Are you telling me or aren't you?

She   Two weeks ago, the third time I went to the superstore. If you're not interested, say so and that will be the end of it. (*Silence.*) It's just I saw the same car and the same man. (**The Husband** *looks at her.*) The same car and the same man as the previous time.

The Husband   He must have a house nearby, like us.

She   What do you think, I just happened to meet up with the same car driven by the same man?

The Husband   Isn't that what you're saying?

She   The car was parked and the man was signalling to me.

The Husband   Oh.

She (*mocking him*)   Oh. The same as before.

The Husband   The same, I don't believe it.

She   Exactly the same.

The Husband   You mean that between the first and the second time no one had taken any notice of him and he was still there, waiting? Even more unshaven, I suppose.

She   I had already decided not to tell you, I'm a fool for having told you. You and your jokes.

The Husband   And how did you react?

She   Forget it.

The Husband   Isn't it a bit strange to meet up with the same vehicle and the same person in the same place and in the same situation?

She   You bet it's strange and I didn't like it at all, and what's more, it's not my imagination.

The Husband   Are you sure it was the same man?

She   He looked just as pathetic. He wasn't badly dressed.

The Husband   And what did you do?

She   Passed him by. Feeling . . . I don't know how to explain it.

The Husband   You're not going to explain it to me.

She   I'm convinced I shouldn't have told you about it now either.

The Husband   Either you were confused or there must be some logical explanation.

She   I suppose so. Confused, I wasn't confused.

The Husband   Maybe you should have stopped.

She   Maybe; I was afraid to. With that fear of not quite understanding where you are.

The Husband   In any case it's not such a big deal.

She   It is what it is.

The Husband   Have you ever heard of the word 'coincidence'?

The Husband *tries to initiate a caress.* **She** *rejects him.*

She   Leave me alone.

The Husband   I'll do the shopping.

She   I'll go.

The Husband   Why?

She   I need to get used to it.

The Husband   Let's not talk about it any more. I know. For instance, just suppose . . .

She   What?

The Husband (*without any form of conviction*)   The man and the car. Suppose someone kept throwing drawing-pins on the road. The poor beggar had his tyres punctured on two occasions.

She   Did they ever puncture your tyres?

The Husband   Mine, no.

She   And don't you drive by the same place? Don't be absurd. It's as if you think I'm some kind of idiot.

The Husband   Don't get upset. I'm not the one who thinks anyone is an idiot.

She *has begun to write on a scrap of paper.*

She   You make me nervous.

The Husband   All the time.

She   You see? (*He laughs discreetly, without malevolence.* **She** *relaxes.*) That's right, laugh.

The Husband   And what do you want me to do?

The Husband *transfers his tools to the table which* **She** *has cleared.*

She (*referring to what she is writing*)   I must have left something out and I'll remember it when I get back. (*Pause.* **She** *seems as though her mind were elsewhere.* **She** *takes one of the sharp tools that is on the table, the chisel, and handles it without looking at it.*) I don't know what's wrong with me.

The Husband (*distracted*)   What's wrong with you?

She   I don't know. (*Pause.*) I get bored. (*Pause.*) And you make me nervous, but I should be used to that by now.

The Husband   You like your work.

She   I liked it before. I don't dislike it. That's not it.

The Husband   Right.

She   Obsessions.

The Husband   I didn't say that.

She   You think it.

The Husband   Are we back to that again?

She   I'm going, I don't know why I'm not doing anything.

The Husband   Turning forty is not so awful.

She (*who was already moving, now stopping*)   What did you say?

The Husband Nothing.

She I don't have a problem with being forty.

The Husband I did.

She It didn't show.

The Husband Just as well.

She Of course, with you, nothing ever shows.

The Husband Forget it.

She I don't have a problem with being forty. What kind of problem could I possibly have? Everything is the same now as it was ten years ago.

The Husband Just as bad.

She Just the same, without adjectives. I don't feel like doing anything. It's something else. It's not my age.

The Husband Go to the doctor.

She Just listen to me . . . I feel fine.

The Husband That doesn't mean anything.

She I know that. I can't be bothered with the doctor. He'll just prescribe vitamins.

The Husband And why not?

She It's not that I'm exactly depressed, either. It's not depression. Or that I'm forty.

The Husband Then it must be the day.

She I don't know why I'm talking to you about it. It's not just today. I've been like this for months. You're happy, aren't you?

The Husband Me?

She I know you are. A few problems at work; but apart from that, happy.

The Husband   Where are you getting this from?

She   Some day, I would like to see you scream at me.

The Husband   Get a move on!

She *puts on a thick casual coat.*

She   I would prefer it that way.

The Husband   Don't get on my nerves.

She   Really.

The Husband   Did you write the cigarettes on the list?

She   One scream, I don't know, just for a change.

The Husband   In this family, having one to do the screaming is enough.

She *grabs the same bag that she has emptied. In the other hand,* **She** *holds the chisel.*

She   A good row that would leave me refreshed, and not now, which is like shouting into the wind. I'm taking the keys, goodbye.

The Husband   Hey, the chisel!

She   Huh?

The Husband   I need it.

She (*staring at the tool which she is holding*)   I didn't realise.

The Husband   I'm using it.

She *leaves it on the table and departs. A distracted glance to the outside which awaits her.*

She   The day is still cloudy and it doesn't look as if it'll change, for better or for worse. These are the worst days.

The Husband   Here inside, it's beginning to warm up. Are you sure you'd prefer to do the shopping?

She   Yes, it'll be fun. I wrote down the cigarettes.

The Husband   Are you a bit more relaxed?

She   As relaxed as possible. Nothing's wrong or will go wrong, this afternoon.

She *leaves. Darkness.*

In the darkness, only the face of a man can be seen.

The Man   This afternoon, once again a marvellous afternoon.
And the damp cold in your bones.
Cold, how wonderful it is to know it's cold. Knowing.
Without a scarf.
The thick sky, solid, as if it were about to fall.
Those are not imposing clouds . . . I remember, we used to call them Wagnerian clouds.
Those clouds that moved towards us, that evening, then, thirty years?, almost thirty years ago.
A memory of yours.
This afternoon's sky, so different. Equally marvellous, too.
Or more so.
Seeing it that way, that's your gift.
A scarf, or better still, a vest.
Always without a vest.
Not wearing a vest doesn't mean you're young any more, but you don't wear it and the cold gets into your bones more easily.
Those clouds moving . . . What simplicity.
The wet road, some hedges, the drizzle that stops and now starts again, the closed sky: beauty.
Beauty without excuses that you can still see, hear, smell . . .
That should not last.
Paradise will not last.
Freed to the exterior shadows, where there is nothing.
Not even pain or longing.
Not yet. Not at the moment. Being here.
Here, waiting.
Now, your job.

Taking advantage of everything. The obsession with not wasting a single crumb.

Taking advantage of the cool breeze that hits your neck.

Taking advantage of your numb feet, of your hands numb from the cold.

Taking advantage of the fact that there is a job to complete: helping with it.

I hope it's done.

Perhaps later, explaining your gift to them, but there won't be any time.

The wet asphalt glistening just for you.

From the day, not long ago, when you had received the gift, from the day that face was met again.

From that day on there is nothing more.

It doesn't matter.

At times, burning with fever, suddenly embarrassed.

You take the hand, you encourage, you push.

Why not? So there's a job to be done.

During this marvellous afternoon, these final wonderful days.

Looking at the gift, a job, this word of comfort.

An unstable word of comfort, which nevertheless allows you to be here, almost happy, on this selfish afternoon.

Understanding finally the leaden colour of the sky, the trembling of the hedges, the hardness of the asphalt . . .

Understanding, above all, this damp cold that gets to your bones, that makes your sickly body shiver.

The illness.

The sentence that sharpens the senses, that allows you to understand, that allows you to be here, patient and expectant.

That still doesn't prevent you from being able to listen for those sounds you most anticipate.

That still . . . I would say that . . . that still allows me to listen for the sound of a car as it drives nearer, at first far off, barely a slight noise, and then, immediately, the rumble of an engine getting louder and louder, dissolving the panic, at least for a while, that spurs me to work, to resolve the waiting, to try again.

Perhaps it will happen this afternoon, in the course of this marvellous afternoon.
Perhaps.
I am signalling.
And yes, the car is coming to a stop.

II

The light comes up, grey, as we hear a car approaching. A road. An expensive car parked on one side. Next to it, in the middle of the road, **The Man** *signals with his arms. Ahead, coming to a stop, the car that we heard, a small car.* **She** *is at the wheel.* **She** *has yet to turn off the engine.* **She** *remains there, staring at* **The Man**. *He smiles, affably, and does not move.* **She** *continues to look at him, rigidly.* **The Man** *takes a few steps towards her and* **She**, *instinctively, checks that the door of her vehicle is locked and that it cannot be opened from the outside.*

The Man   Thank you for stopping. Excuse me.

She   What do you want?

The Man   I don't know what's wrong with my car.

She (*turns off the engine*)   What do you want?

The Man   I'll hardly be any trouble. If you could drop me off where there's a phone . . .

She   Why are you doing this?

The Man   What?

She   It's the third time.

The Man   The car broke down. I hardly know anything about car mechanics.

She   Tell me!

The Man   I am telling you.

She   Tell me!

The Man   I don't understand you, calm down.

She   I'm calmer than you'd like me to be!

The Man   My car broke down. I need to call the mechanic and have him come here. If you could give me a lift, I'd appreciate it; if not, there's not much I can do.

He turns his back to her, walking away. **She** *then opens the door of her vehicle and looks outside.*

She   Wait! (*He stops.*) Do you think it will be so easy?

The Man (*looks at her again*)   Why are you angry?

She   Don't you know?

The Man   If you don't want to take me, no one's forcing you.

She *suddenly decides to get out of the car.* **She** *is not wearing the coat she was wearing when she left the house. The cold catches her unawares when she is out in the open.*

She   It won't be so easy for you. I've stopped and I'm not leaving before I find out what's going on.

The Man   I don't understand.

She   Of course you do.

The Man   Go back to your car, you'll catch cold.

She   I'm not at all afraid of you. If your intention was to frighten me, I'm telling you I'm not afraid. But I want to know why you're doing it.

The Man   I'm not frightening anyone.

She   Why are you doing it?

The Man   Go away. You're not wearing a coat and I'm sure you don't like the cold.

She   Who are you?

The Man   Forget it. Look, I'm not in the mood to get into an argument.

She   Then why are you following me?

The Man   Me?

She   This is the third time I've seen you.

The Man   The third time?

She   Yes.

The Man   When? I don't remember. Excuse me, I don't remember you.

She   That's three times.

The Man   Have you and I met before?

She   It cannot be a coincidence.

The Man   Do we know each other?

She   Do we know each other?

The Man   I don't remember you. I'm sorry. I have a bad memory for faces. Don't be offended.

She   Of course we haven't met. Did you get frightened, when you saw me stop my car? Does it bother you that I got out of my car?

The Man   Are you feeling all right?

She   Did you think you could frighten me as many times as you wanted, and I wouldn't dare face up to you?

The Man   Why should you face up to me?

She   I am facing up to you.

The Man   You're sticking your face right in mine. And in this cold you're going to catch pneumonia.

She   Very funny. You like joking around?

The Man   Joking around?

She   Yes, are you some kind of joker?

The Man   Me? I don't know. As much as anyone else, I suppose.

She   It was a joke, then?

The Man   What was?

She   At least say it was a joke.

The Man   Listen, why don't you just go away?

She   A stupid joke. And now that I've confronted you, you're sorry.

The Man   About what?

She   But, why me? Why did you choose me?

The Man   There must be some sense in what you're saying.

She   You chose me out of the blue.

The Man   You must be confusing me.

She   No, not out of the blue.

The Man   You must be confusing me.

She   It's too strange to be a joke. It isn't a joke. What is it, then?

The Man   I'm telling you you're confused. It happens sometimes.

She   I haven't confused you. You or your car.

The Man   Didn't you stop to help me? Did you stop because you've confused me with someone else?

She   I'm not moving until you tell me.

The Man   Put your coat on.

She   I don't want to put my coat on, leave me alone, will you!

The Man   I don't know what to say. Whatever I say seems to bother you.

She   You're not telling the truth.

The Man   I'm not trying to bother you. I had a breakdown and I needed to stop the first car that passed by.

She   You're not telling the truth.

The Man   This is a deserted road. A deserted little road; not a soul comes here.

She   Exactly, not a soul comes here. That's why seeing you here three times can't be a coincidence.

The Man   It's the first time we've met, if I'm not mistaken.

She   And even less seeing you in these circumstances.

The Man   Here? On this road?

She   Of course.

The Man   Impossible.

She   And in these circumstances.

The Man   Here, completely impossible. It's a mistake, I thought it was.

She   The three times, dressed the same.

The Man   A mistake, you can be sure of it.

She   You and your car.

The Man   I'm an ordinary man, I'm easily confused with other people.

She   The other times you signalled to me.

The Man   What?

She   Signalled for me to stop.

The Man   Signalled for you to stop?

She   Yes.

The Man   Really?

She   You're a shameless bastard.

The Man   Calm down, wait.

She   You're making me repeat what you already know and you're pretending to be surprised.

The Man   A man like me, three times counting today . . . Counting today?

She   Not a man like you, it was you.

The Man   Three times, on this road, someone like me signalled for you to stop?

She   On this road and at this exact spot in the road.

The Man   Really?

She   Perhaps the first time I should have stopped. Perhaps everything happened because of that. Is that why?

The Man   It doesn't make sense.

She   I was probably wrong to leave a person asking for help alone on a deserted road.

The Man   Like a bad dream, I suppose.

She   I got frightened. Today I should be even more frightened, but the indignation . . . The indignation . . . And especially . . .

The Man   Yes.

She   If I'd just driven by, afterwards I wouldn't have been able to stand it. Just the thought that I could run into you again another day . . . Was worse than stopping and demanding an explanation.

The Man   It's a pity I can't offer you any explanation. At least, any explanation of the kind you're expecting.

She   I'm not leaving until you give me an explanation.

The Man   I understand your situation. You're quite understandably upset. I am really sorry. It's just that . . . I won't be able to help you.

She   Oh yes you will.

The Man   I won't be able to help you in the way you expect. I'll try and convince you that it's been a mistake.

She   You won't fool me.

The Man   It's all I can do. You live nearby.

She   I have a house not far from here. We come here on weekends.

The Man   And you often drive down this road.

She   I don't have any choice but to drive down it. You must have known that.

The Man   But I live a good distance from here. Hundreds of kilometres between your house . . . and mine.

She   So what?

The Man   Today is the first time I've driven round here.

She   No it's not.

The Man   The first time, I assure you.

She   I saw you.

The Man   A case of confusion, there's no other way around it.

She   A lie. You're lying.

The Man   To be more exact, fifteen years ago, let's say, about fifteen years ago, I visited this area.

She   I'm not interested in fifteen years ago.

The Man   There weren't any housing developments or a road. It was different.

She   Why did you come today?

The Man   I didn't. I'm passing through. And all of a sudden, the breakdown.

She   I have not gone mad. I was not hallucinating. I don't believe you.

The Man   I cannot offer you any other explanation.

She   I'm not inventing it. I've talked to my husband about it.

The Man   I'm sorry. Do I look like I would want to frighten anyone, me? I doubt it. And stupid jokes are not my thing. It doesn't matter. What reason would I have to bother you, if I don't even know you?

She   That's what I would like to know.

The Man   No reason. Not one. It's nonsense! Don't you understand? (*Pause.*) Go on, off with you. In any case, you must be feeling calmer now.

She   Don't assume anything.

The Man   You're freezing, off you go. A mistake, a coincidence, that's all.

She   No, no.

The Man   It won't happen again.

She   Are you refusing to explain yourself?

The Man   I've done what I can.

She   If I meet up with you again one day . . .

The Man   You won't meet up with me again.

She   I'm not easily frightened, you've already seen that. If I meet up with you again one day . . . I don't like threatening people, I have to defend myself.

The Man   You won't meet up with me again.

She   You'll be the one to decide that.

The Man   When I do manage to get out of here, I still have to drive between three and four hours. A long distance. I don't plan on returning. When I saw the detour, I thought it would be a good shortcut, that it would save time. Once I manage to get out of here, it's hardly likely I shall ever have the occasion to return. Probably never again.

She   You're a very good liar.

The Man   No I'm not.

She   Yes you are. (*Pause.*) What should I do?

The Man   Go away.

She   There's a cafeteria. It's not far. If you really need to call a mechanic, there's probably a telephone there.

The Man   Right.

She   I'll take you.

The Man   You'll take me with you?

She   I suppose so. What else can I do?

The Man   Do you believe me?

She   No. You wanted me to stop twice before today.

The Man (*smiles*)   My God.

She   But in any case, what choice do I have?

The Man   I really don't know.

She   I suppose you can't harm me.

The Man   Of course I can't and of course I don't want to.

She   It won't clear anything up. But, I'll take you.

The Man   Thank you.

The Man *goes over to lock his car.*

She   It's so cold . . .

The Man   You must be freezing and it's all my fault.

She   Aren't you cold?

The Man   I've got more clothes on.

She   The humidity soaks through your clothes and you must have been waiting for a while on the road.

The Man   A good while.

The Man *returns to her side.*

She   Waiting for me to arrive.

The Man   Waiting for someone to arrive.

She   Get in.

The Man   On one condition.

She   What?

The Man   A cafeteria, is that where we're going?

She   Yes.

The Man   I'll buy you a coffee.

She   A beer.

The Man   You'll need something hot.

She   Beer. I don't like coffee, I like beer.

The Man   Do you drink a lot?

She   More than I should.

The Man   Why?

She   Why not? No reason. Get in the car. It's just a minute away, we'll be there in no time.

Darkness.

In the darkness, only the face of a woman can be seen.

The Woman   He'll take a while to get here, because he's patient.

And when he does get here, finally, he'll be alone. Why is he helping me?

I don't ask.

No explanations; never; that is what has saved us.

A lie. I did, I spoke.

And he's helping me. What is it that moves him, since love . . . ?

Love, that ignoble word.

Pink hearts and sky-blue ribbons: miseries.

Ridiculous clichés repeated and accepted for centuries.

I could give a speech on the topic.

A speech as unbearable as my obsessions.

How much longer will I have to wait?

I am not a patient person.

Passion is brief, perhaps, but not patient.

Better to know that this illness has an end, that this anguish will have an end.

That the joy will be extinguished, but also the pain.

What joy?

Yes, the joy. All right, the joy, the crazed emotions.

But never to arrive, not even then, there where you want to arrive.

Anxiety does not allow it, serenity disappears.

Converted into a poor vulnerable animal.

Who's coming in?

It's still not him.

So few people come in, they have so few customers, this afternoon . . .

It's not a pleasant day, no one dares go out on the road.

A deserted interior, four poor souls controlling each other.

Not a single pair of lovers.

Not a single pair to give a mistaken name to their desires.

My parents loved each other.

With tenderness, until they died.

What was that?

I've never seen anything that looked so much like love.

What was it?

Nothing is certain.

That kind of serenity.

To go from the serenity of one's parents to the serenity of a husband.

But no, between one thing and another, that.

A calm, quiet husband, and that whole thing had already happened.

It had awakened, freed, driven me, and then, him and his protection.

Why not? The comfort of letting him do it.

Until today. I use him and perhaps he uses me.

Not at all dissonant, and not a single excessively high note.

Perhaps, in him, at the beginning, passion.

Perhaps yes, in him.

If he had a problem, I don't share his sorrow.

I know what I'm talking about, everything comes and goes.

The passion burns out and in the end it's extinguished.

The only consolation, knowing that it is inevitable, that it will end with the flame going out.

No, please, I don't want that to happen, no!

Calm down, it's also part of the process: rejecting the remedy.

Calm down. Invent it as you can: calm down.

Where did this song come from?

This stupid sentimental tune?

On the other side of the glass a car stops. It's not his.

I didn't realise there was music.

It's not his, but he's the one getting out of the car now. And of course, he's not alone.

He's not alone, he's not alone, he's not alone.

How awful, I'll have to associate his appearance with this sentimental, sloppy music that is playing here inside.

I'll always hold on to . . . it's funny, it's ridiculous, what a disaster.

Accept it, I'll always hold on to the memory of this music.

III

The lights come up and music is heard. Very close together, two small, mass-produced plastic tables, with seats attached. Behind them, steamed-up windows. One of the tables is covered with the remains from a meal: paper cups, dirty, crumpled paper napkins, cigarette butts in plastic ashtrays. On the other table there are two cups of coffee, one of them empty and the other half full. The seat in front of the cups is occupied by **The Woman**, *dressed with severity and elegance. She has just finished speaking and leans over the half-full cup of coffee; she stirs it with a spoon and takes a sip.. She closes her eyes and swallows hard.* **She** *and* **The Man** *arrive. He carries a beer and a white coffee on a brightly coloured tray. He sweeps away the leftovers making a mess on the free table and puts down his own utensils. They take off their coats and sit down.* **The Woman**, *at the other small table, is seated with her back to them.*

She   Can't they turn the music down?

The Man   At least it's warm. You need to lighten up. This kind of muzak doesn't bother me.

She   Plastic music, I call it. Just right for a cafeteria where everything is plastic, even the coffee and the beer.

The Man   Plastic?

She   That's one way of describing it.

The Man   Oh, of course.

She   I'll only stay a moment, it's getting late.

The Man   Thank you . . . and sorry to have bothered you.

She   The telephone must be inside, where the toilets are.

The Man   I'll manage. I plan to phone a reliable mechanic . . . Even though it's a weekend he'll come and pick up the car.

She   I have to do some shopping. There's a superstore. (*Pause.*) A reliable mechanic, you said?

The Man   Yes, don't worry.

She   Near enough. The mechanic lives near here, of course.

The Man   Pretty near here.

She   Near here? But you don't know anybody around here. Don't you live three or four hours away by car? And you don't know the area, you said you had never been back, that the last time was fifteen years ago. You're lying.

The Man   Wait, don't get carried away.

She   I knew it. Now you can't deny it: you're lying.

The Man   Wait, let me explain.

She   Who are you?

The Man   Let's not start, you're too suspicious, you twist everything around.

She   I'm sick of these stories.

The Man   Let me speak. I'm a man who takes precautions. There's a service network, wherever you go . . . You pay a small fee, you never get stranded, there's always a reliable mechanic nearby, if you call the emergency number.

She   You know all too well how to wriggle your way out of it, but you don't fool me. You've been caught.

The Man   What are you talking about? I'm telling you the truth, really.

She   You never fooled me. But, why? Why don't you tell me once and for all what you want?

The Woman, *seated, back to back, practically rubbing against her, turns and looks at* **The Man**.

The Woman   What are you doing here?

The Man (*relieved*)   Oh, hello. Hello.

He stands politely. **The Woman** *still does not move from where she is.*

The Woman   I heard your voice.

The Man   How are you?

The Woman   I'm managing.

The Man   My car broke down. This lady picked me up and brought me here. I'm going to call a mechanic.

The Woman   Lucky you found someone nice. (*Gets up, holding her coffee cup.*) Can I join you?

The Man   Oh, of course. (*To her.*) Do you mind?

She (*without looking up*)   No.

The Man *lets* **The Woman** *by and she sits down beside him, in front of her. Now, the two women are facing each other.*

The Woman   Thank you. I hope you weren't talking about anything important.

The Man   We've just met.

The Woman   So? Excuse me. I was just passing the time of day. These gloomy afternoons . . . I appreciate the company. There shouldn't be any afternoons like this.

The Man   They're also quite beautiful, these afternoons.

The Woman   You can't be serious! (*To her, complicitly.*) Did you hear him? Do you think there's anything nice about a cold and rainy afternoon?

She   Nothing.

The Woman (*delighted, to* **The Man**)   You see? (*To her.*) Oh, beer! You're having a beer, what a good idea. I've already had two coffees and I won't sleep tonight. A good beer, that's what I needed. One or two. Beer goes to my head, I don't deny it, but, so what? Doesn't it go to your head?

She   It depends.

The Woman   With me, it always does. And frankly, there's nothing more I could wish for. It goes to your head, it relaxes you, maybe you talk too much . . . Becoming moderately tipsy from beer, three or four bottles, perks up your day when you need it.

She   I don't need to get drunk.

The Woman   I'm talking about me, of course! I don't mind recognising my faults.

The Man (*jokingly*)   Oh, don't you? Do you have a lot?

The Woman   None; really, none. I'm a very good girl, you already know me.

The Man   Yes.

The Woman   Or perhaps I'm over-indulgent. When you're slightly drunk you don't do any harm to anyone and it's a way of letting yourself go. I don't consider it a fault.

The Man   Hey, you're the one who said you know how to recognise your own faults.

The Woman   I'm contradicting myself, aren't I? And I'm not letting the two of you talk, I've interrupted your conversation. Excuse me.

The Man   No, in fact I need to make that phone call. I won't calm down until I've made that call.

She   I need to go.

The Man   One moment. Wait a moment. I'll make that call and I'll be right back.

She   What do I have to gain from waiting for you?

The Man   Don't you want an explanation?

She   Will you give me one?

The Man   Yes.

The Woman   What are you two talking about?

She (*without paying her any attention*)   A real explanation?

The Man   A real one, I promise.

She   You admit it wasn't the first time?

The Man   I'm going to make that call. I'll just be a second.

She   I'll wait for you. I don't know why, but I'll wait.

The Man (*to* **The Woman**)   Talk to her. She's done me a huge favour and I'm indebted to her.

The Woman   She won't be short of conversation. I was so bored and you've saved my afternoon. On the contrary, if I go on too much, stop me.

The Man   I'll be a second.

He walks away from the women, leaving them alone.

The Woman (*watching him go*)   Men are different. Don't you think?

She   Is he a good friend of yours?

The Woman   Poor thing.

She   Are you good friends?

The Woman   More or less. I've had few close friends over the years.

She   That's a surprise. You're such an extrovert.

The Woman   Ha, do I seem that way to you? No, it's today, it's this afternoon, it's the two coffees. And because of you, you seem nice. I'm not an extrovert at all. It must be the moment.

She   Is home far from here?

The Woman   Not really. And yours?

She   We have a little place for the weekends, in the housing development.

The Woman   Before they began construction on the development, mine was the only house. No, I don't live very far away.

She   I meant his home.

The Woman   His home?

She   Is his home far from here?

The Woman   Where do you expect him to live?

She   He told me it was very far away, three or four hours by car. Three hours aren't the same as four. I need to know if it's three or four.

The Woman (*disinterested*)   Right.

She   But it was hardly a surprise for the two of you to bump into each other.

The Woman   Why should it have been?

She   Well, if he lives far from here, as he assured me. If he lives far from here, you can't see each other all that often.

The Woman   We see each other occasionally. Yes, we see each other, of course. Are you all right?

She   Yes.

The Woman   Don't worry about it, dear. Men's obsessions.

She   It's a strange situation . . . He's been lying to me and I don't know why.

The Woman   Forget about it. Does one lie matter to you?

She   Where does he live?

The Woman   A lie doesn't matter. Attitudes are more important. Sometimes you lie out of fondness for someone, one can also lie out of fondness, it's not necessarily true that behind every lie there's a hostile attitude. A long time ago, such a long time ago . . . Seventeen or eighteen years begin to be real years, and they're gone in a flash. As though there was nothing in between.

She   Don't you want to tell me?

The Woman   There's nothing else I'd like better. Seventeen long years ago, now. I fell in love.

She (*impatiently*)   Oh, really?

The Woman   Have you ever been in love before?

She   Everybody's been in love at some time.

The Woman   More than once?

She   Possibly.

The Woman   Really? Right. Well, I can't say the same for me. That was the only time I fell in love.

She   Excuse me, just one question.

The Woman   What?

She   If you could answer one question . . .

The Woman   Yes, yes, ask away. Are you bothered by my secrets?

She   No. One question, that's all.

The Woman   Go ahead.

She   Where does your friend live?

The Woman   Where does he live? I don't think I have my address book with me. Where does he live? It's on the tip of my tongue. What difference does it make? When he gets back, he'll tell us himself. Now, what was I telling you? About the time I fell in love.

She   You really don't remember?

The Woman I remember everything. Moment by moment, day by day. It was the first time I really fell in love. It was the only time in my life I fell in love. I'm boring you.

She Perhaps I should go.

The Woman You told him you'd wait.

She In any case, perhaps I should go.

The Woman It's my fault, I'm going on and on and boring you.

She No, no you're not.

The Woman He'll be right back. We should ask him where the hell he lives. If I'm boring you, tell me.

She Don't worry.

The Woman Whiling away the time chatting about love at the age of forty, just fancy that.

She How do you know my age?

The Woman Mine. I'm forty. You too?

She Yes.

The Woman Then you'll understand. At forty life hasn't ended. Your love life, I mean. And sex. Sex is very important. Nothing's ended. We have years and years ahead of us. I should have been able to fall in love again; who says I can't? The problem . . . the problem is that I've never stopped being in love.

Pause.

She (*ill-at-ease and non-committal*) Really?

The Woman You understand me, don't you?

She I don't know.

The Woman I fell in love when I was twenty-two. I felt myself fall in love as though it were a slap in the face. And they realised it. I couldn't hide it! I was completely absorbed by them. It was unbearable. I felt so ashamed, I didn't dare take any kind of initiative . . . And I was completely absorbed by them! It was a cordial relationship, our friendship grew, although for the time being it was one friendship among many . . . A normal relationship but cold, almost colder than normal. Between friends it's normal to establish a certain level of physical contact, don't you think? A hand that rests on your shoulder or grabs your hand . . . Details. So, that was it. That's how things went on for months. At night I cried. I was all burning inside and I didn't have any other choice, something that I had only rarely done, I had no other choice but to masturbate. I masturbated and I cried and I felt humiliated.

She (*interrupting*)   He probably should have been back by now.

The Woman   I didn't know how to accept my situation as natural. I wasn't capable of taking the initiative, nor was I capable of accepting my nocturnal practices as a natural outlet . . .

She   I think he should have been back.

The Woman   Boys are more used to it; they see masturbation differently. At least that's how it was in my time.

She   Don't you think so?

The Woman   Pardon? Sorry, what did you say?

She   Your friend. His call to the mechanic is taking an awfully long time.

The Woman   Is it?

She   I can't understand what he's doing.

The Woman   Maybe there was someone in front of him.

She   The cafeteria is practically empty. I don't think so.

The Woman   He left us just a moment ago.

She He should have been here already.

The Woman He'll be back right away.

She I don't have a lot of time.

The Woman On an afternoon like this? Why should you be in a hurry on an afternoon like this?

She I have to do some shopping.

The Woman You still have time. Of course, unless you feel uncomfortable here with me. Perhaps I've forced my conversation on you in an abusive sort of way.

She It's not that.

The Woman Isn't it? Really?

She No . . .

The Woman My story isn't boring you?

She It's your . . . intimacy.

The Woman You could call it that.

She Perhaps you shouldn't have told me. I don't know if it's any of my business.

The Woman Why not? I feel comfortable with you. And it's not so important.

She You would know, of course.

The Woman Everyone has their stories, and they're all similar. Don't you have a story?

She Me? No.

The Woman No?

She Yes, one . . . I got married . . . One.

The Woman Before you told me you'd fallen in love on more than one occasion. It's only happened to me once. I have very little experience, certainly much less than you.

She   I don't know what to say.

The Woman   But my experience is special, grant me a bit of originality. Or perhaps not? Perhaps I'm wrong. Later on, they got into the habit of calling me. There was some progress. But it was worse. I became dependent on the phone calls. The obsession with the telephone. The telephone is a mortal weapon. I'm not the only one who says so, everyone who's ever gone through it says so. Has it never happened to you?

She   I don't think so.

The Woman   You've never been afraid of the telephone?

She   It's an object.

The Woman   Really? Never?

She   Oh, at the most, the odd idiot who won't speak to you when you pick up the receiver . . .

The Woman   And finally, I was so desperate, one day, on the phone, while they were talking to me about something, I interrupted, I couldn't go on any longer, and I declared my love, I said I'd fallen in love.

Pause. **She** *looks at* **The Woman** *in a different way, rigidly.*

She (*trying to adopt a trivial tone*)   When the devil will he finish talking to the mechanic?

The Woman   I'd fallen in love.

She (*impulsively*)   A long time ago, was it?

The Woman   Seventeen or eighteen years ago. Maybe eighteen.

She (*lightly*)   What stories. (*From now on* **She** *does not look* **The Woman** *in the eye.*) I'm married and I have two daughters.

The Woman   Probably eighteen.

She (*suddenly loquacious*)   I had gone out with other men, but my husband was different. I didn't know if I should get married. I wasn't sure about bringing up children, for example.

The Woman   They arranged to meet me.

She   And the man who was to be my husband appeared and he didn't leave me any other choice. I hardly even gave it any thought. There I was, married. I work and I like my job, but I always feel like going home. He still loves me and I still love him. I don't know if I should say this. Maybe I'm wildly in love with him, you see. I think I might love him more than I love my daughters.

The Woman   I'm in love, as well.

She   Oh, really?

The Woman   With the person I was telling you about, the person in question.

She   The story isn't over?

The Woman   Not at all.

She   Have you gone on seeing this person? (*Trivially.*) Did you get married?

The Woman   Of course not. How would you expect us to get married?

She   Don't tell me he hasn't been too long on the phone.

The Woman   I stopped seeing them. Five months and we stopped seeing each other. The only time in my life I've fallen in love.

She   An old story.

The Woman   No. I'm in love with this person.

She   After seventeen or eighteen years without seeing someone it's impossible.

The Woman   I am.

She I can't stay, I'm going.

The Woman Wait, I haven't told you what happened. Just a minute.

She I can't.

The Woman I'm about to finish. I told you how it began, I told you that it ended, but I've got to tell you the best part.

She There's no need.

The Woman Let me. (*Pause.*) We had a date. At their house. And they were alone. The door opened and we held each other. We made love.

She (*lightly*) A happy ending.

The Woman For five months, until they left me. Lied to me and left me.

She Five months of happiness.

The Woman Five months of fulfilment. Happiness, no.

She Is that it, then?

The Woman The room where we made love for the first time. I close my eyes and I can see it. There was a white crocheted quilt. The bed was not very big. There was a small antique cupboard, made of black wood, with a mirror. There was a child's clock, with a small figure that moved its eyes to the rhythm of the seconds, and had clock hands for arms. I remember the tick-tock of that clock, the rumpled quilt which had fallen on the floor, our image reflected in the mirror of the cupboard. I shall always remember it. I'm still in love.

She (*sarcastically*) Is that it?

The Woman And afterwards, they lied to me, but that's not what matters.

She Have you finished?

The Woman Perhaps now, yes.

She   I didn't understand your story.

Unexpectedly, **She** *stands up, grabs her coat and leaves.* **The Woman** *remains still. She has not finished drinking her coffee.* **She***, on the other hand, had been drinking beer.* **The Woman** *tastes the coffee, makes a grimace of disgust, and pushes it away. Pause.* **The Man** *comes over to her.*

The Man   She left.

The Woman   Yes.

The Man   You talked.

The Woman   Well, talk . . .

The Man   And . . . ?

The Woman   God knows.

The Man   How are you doing?

The Woman   Yes, better.

The Man   And now what?

The Woman   What?

The Man   Shall we go, perhaps?

The Woman   Where?

The Man   Home.

The Woman   Home.

The Man   All right?

The Woman   Are you tired?

The Man   Sort of.

The Woman   You are, aren't you?

The Man   Not really.

The Woman   There are still things to do.

The Man   All right.

The Woman   Will you be able to?

The Man   What do you think?

The Woman   I don't know.

The Man   Well, of course I'll be able to.

The Woman   Sure?

The Man   Let's go.

The Woman   Thank you.

The Man   You don't have to thank *me*.

Darkness.

In the darkness, only the face of **The Husband** *can be seen.*

The Husband   I don't need to say thank you for it.
To anyone.
I did it by myself, with the years.
Hold her, keep her, see her, look at her, feel her, listen to her.
Sometimes, spy on her, as well.
And wait for her, like I'm waiting now.
With my anguished affection, a shame renewed each day.
My obscenity, the vice that is born and ends in me, without her knowing.
I hope she isn't aware of this dependence: so that things won't change. They will not change. Work and persevere, and then they don't change.
Work the way I like to.
The wood has knots, but you have to move the tool lightly over them, even more skilfully, without losing control.
It's turning out the way I wanted.
The skill is acquired over the years.
I dominate the chisel and I dig it into the wood with pleasure, with certainty, precision.
I see the knot, I go up to it, I rub my fingers over it, I study its difficulty and then I begin to work on it.
Happiness.

There have to be knots, to love the knots.
I'm almost finished.
A way of waiting.
And delaying the stupid anxiety.
From the first day, from the first exchange of words.
Until this very day.
The excitement of the beginning, the passion of the start,
not converted into habit, the way it has to be.
Transformed into worry, jealousy, anxiety.
But she doesn't know and she won't know.
Not to ruin it.
The years go by and it isn't ruined.
She takes me or leaves me, sings or grumbles: it's her.
Damn her.
Damn her and the moment I met her.
Bound to her, until today, bound to her.
Careful. The wood, careful.
I think I've learned.
Always attentive and waiting, without being able to free
myself.
But what difference does it make?
Humbled in front of the vice that joins me to her, this
abominable, absurd, ridiculous, feeling that joins me to her.
But what difference does it make?
No one knows.
I've kept it hidden.
As if nothing happened, as if it were a story of an alliance
endured with resignation.
Because my hands have learned to dominate the wood
effortlessly.
To work it, smooth it down, give it meaning and purpose.
Like right now, now that I've finished it and I am happy.
Control, dominate, transform the anguish.
Happy. I've finished. Just in time. She's coming.
She'll put the key into the lock and she'll come in.
Her blessed, aggressive bad mood, perhaps. It doesn't
matter to me, my job, not giving myself away.
I'll hide my craftsman's pride. My craftsman's anxiety.
She puts the key into the lock.

As always, I'll hide the feelings that could be disturbing.
She's coming in.
What could break the equilibrium – a curious word – the
equilibrium achieved over the years.
She's coming in, she's coming in at last, and I am happy.

IV

*The light comes up and we are at the single-family home of the first
scene.* **The Husband** *has been putting his tools away, but he has
not finished doing so, and looks up to see her enter, as* **She** *returns from
being away, with her coat on.*

She (*excited*)   I'm happy.

The Husband   Are you? Did you find everything you
needed?

She (*laughs*)   No. Nothing.

She *takes her coat off.*

The Husband   What do you mean, nothing?

She   Nothing. I didn't go shopping.

The Husband   Didn't you?

She   No.

The Husband   What happened to you?

She   What was supposed to happen to me?

The Husband   What did you do?

She   I went for a walk.

The Husband   On an afternoon like this?

She   A walk through the countryside.

The Husband   You?

She   I changed my mind. I'll do the shopping another day.

The Husband   You said it was urgent.

She   Having a good time is more urgent.

The Husband   Yes, of course. And did you have a good time?

She   Perfect. I left the car on the side of the road and got out to stretch my legs. In the fields.

The Husband   In the fields?

She   Yes.

She *grabs a beer, takes off the bottle top, and will go on drinking during the scene.*

The Husband   Another beer?

She   I'm thirsty.

The Husband   The mud didn't dirty your shoes.

She   I was careful. You're awfully observant, when you want to be.

The Husband   Me?

She   I don't mind you being like that.

The Husband   Where did you go?

She   I don't know.

The Husband   What did you see?

She   I wasn't looking. But the cold was stimulating and I've cheered up.

The Husband   I'm glad.

She (*referring to the wooden contraption* **The Husband** *was making*)   Have you finished it?

The Husband   I need to paint it.

She   You've got good hands.

The Husband   Thank you. I'll send you out for a walk every day.

She (*drily*)   No!

The Husband   No?

She   Once is enough.

The Husband   I'm glad you've come home happy.

She   And let's not talk about it any more.

The Husband   All right, we won't talk about it.

She   Of course, it's not hard for you to keep quiet.

The Husband   Do you think so?

She   What do you think?

The Husband   About what?

She   About us. I'd like to know.

The Husband   Let's not complicate our lives.

She   How long has it been, since we met?

The Husband   I can count the years.

She   When *you* were young, did you ever imagine what was going to happen?

The Husband   When we were young . . . Like any young people, right? We thought we could do everything. There was room for everything in life.

She   Oh, be quiet.

The Husband   Didn't you ask me to speak?

She   I don't want you to read the manual to me.

The Husband   And what do you want?

She   Try to imagine. To chat, to be with you. You're my husband.

The Husband   That's right.

She   We've got each other, you know?

The Husband   What's wrong with you?

She   Answer.

The Husband   Yes, that's also the manual, we've got each other. What's wrong with you?

She   You've got me.

The Husband   Where are we? I'm lost.

She   You've never doubted it, surely.

The Husband   What is all this?

She   And you've done well.

The Husband   I don't know what to say.

She   What's so strange about talking? Let's talk. You, too. I'm the one who's always talking. Let's both talk. The heating is working now.

The Husband   You've noticed? You've realised, eh?

She   It's cold outside. Damp and unpleasantly cold.

The Husband   Unpleasant.

She   You would say so.

The Husband   You've already said so. A stimulating cold, you said.

She   Do you have to control what I say?

The Husband   No.

She   It seems like it.

The Husband   No it doesn't.

She   I had a nice time, yes: and I've come home and here it's even better.

The Husband   Now, here, it feels good. It feels nice.
You'll see how good we'll feel here. A little house, just our
size, and where it's nice.

She   A house for the rest of our life.

The Husband   We'll have to fix it up. Bit by bit.

She   You enjoy fixing it up.

The Husband   Yes.

She   But it must mean a lot of work for you.

The Husband   Years of work. It doesn't matter to me,
it's a distraction.

She   Years to fix it up. And then it'll be fixed.

The Husband   I already feel fine here; there's no need to
wait.

She   I feel fine here, too. You've got good hands.

The Husband   It seems like it. Why didn't you do the
shopping?

She   Didn't I tell you?

The Husband   Yes . . .

She   Well?

The Husband   I haven't got any cigarettes.

She   Oh, I'm sorry.

The Husband   I'll go out later and get some.

She   Where will you go?

The Husband   I can just go to the cafeteria.

She   That filthy place.

The Husband   Maybe I'll finish putting away the tools.

She   Wait, we were talking. Don't you feel like it? You and
me here, talking. The girls aren't here.

The Husband　Do you miss them?

She　Not at all. Do you miss them?

The Husband　I haven't stopped to think about it. I don't know. It depends on how you look at it.

She　I don't at all. The girls changed our lives.

The Husband　It usually happens.

She　I'm glad they're not here. We should send them off more often.

The Husband　Send them off.

She　Children are selfish. They don't even realise it. And you always give in.

The Husband　That's one way of looking at it.

She　They should go out on their own. I love them, but they should go out on their own more often. I need . . .

Pause.

The Husband　What were you going to say?

She　What I want is to be with you. With you, without distractions.

The Husband　Really?

She　I said so to somebody not long ago. It slipped out. There are things it seems you shouldn't say. It slipped out and I didn't realise what I was saying and then I realised after I'd said it.

The Husband　What did you say?

She　Don't laugh, that I love you more than the girls.

Pause. **The Husband** *looks at her.*

The Husband　That's not true.

She　Don't you want it to be true?

The Husband   The fact is it's not.

She   It seems ugly to say it, like something that should never be said.

The Husband   You don't understand me.

She   Should I keep quiet, if that's what I think?

The Husband   No.

She   I'm not harming anyone. Not even the girls.

The Husband   What's the matter?

She   With me?

The Husband   Why are you saying these things?

She   And why aren't you saying anything?

The Husband   Anything?

She   Anything nice.

The Husband   Like what?

She   Like what I've said to you.

The Husband   I don't know.

She   Can't you?

The Husband   If I come closer and touch you, you'll say I'm a pain in the neck.

She   Is that a nice thing to say?

The Husband   Words are deceptive.

She   So what?

The Husband *moves closer to her and takes her in his arms.*

The Husband   You're not going to kick me?

She   It was hard for you.

The Husband   It doesn't usually have a successful outcome.

She   Do you like it?

The Husband   I like holding you.

She   That's what I wanted to know.

The Husband   I like it.

Silence. Intimate gestures that become more and more passionate. Perhaps twenty seconds, perhaps half a minute. Then the telephone rings. They stop.

She   I'll get it. (**She** *goes over, and picks up the receiver*.) Hello. (*Pause*.) Hello. (*Pause*.) Hello!

The Husband   No answer?

She   Hello!

She *hangs up abruptly*.

The Husband   It's strange. Maybe you're right, I'll call the phone company, just in case.

She   There's no need.

The Husband   There may be problems with the line.

She   No.

The Husband   Don't you think so?

She   There was someone there, it's not a problem with the phone service.

The Husband   Some pain in the neck.

She   Yes, there was someone on the other end of the line.

The Husband   Someone who's bored.

She   Someone who's having fun.

The Husband   Call it what you will.

She   Someone who doesn't want to leave me alone.

The Husband   Who doesn't want to leave us alone.

She   Me, it's on account of me.

The Husband   Maybe they're calling at random.

She   And before? This is the second time. Before, they even asked for me, they gave you my name.

The Husband   It probably wasn't the same person.

She   It probably was.

The Husband   Who?

She   How should I know?

The Husband   Leave it be, then. Don't get obsessed.

She   What do they want?

The Husband   There's no need to worry about it. It happens to everyone. Don't worry about it.

She   The phone . . .

The Husband   Just forget it.

She   The phone is like . . ., it's like a weapon . . .

The Husband   Don't exaggerate.

She   It is.

The Husband   They didn't say anything to you.

She   No.

The Husband   They didn't threaten you or say anything to you.

She   No.

The Husband   You should never pay any attention to tricks on the phone, even if they threaten you. But they didn't threaten you. It happens to everyone, it happens every day.

She   It doesn't happen every day.

The Husband   But it happens, and no one worries about it. Why should you worry about it? (**She** *is silent.*) You've confused it with what happened on the road, that's why you're worrying about it so much.

She (*jumping up*)   What did you say?

The Husband   You've probably been thinking about it and you've confused one thing with the other.

She   Shut up, that's nonsense.

The Husband   It can't be, I don't want you to get any strange ideas.

She   Will you shut up?

The Husband   It's for your own good.

She (*sarcastically*)   Ha!

The Husband   And since the subject has come up . . .

She   Let's not talk about it any more, there's no point.

The Husband   Since the subject has come up, I know perfectly well why you didn't go shopping.

She   Oh, really? What do you know?

The Husband   Don't be like that, don't get upset.

She   OK then, what do you know?

The Husband   These crazy ideas, I don't know where they come from but we've got to get to the bottom of this and I'm going to help you. OK, I know they're not crazy ideas, I've had them, too.

She   You don't know anything.

The Husband   You didn't go shopping because you didn't dare go there. Admit it: you invented that walk through the countryside. I can see you there, sitting in the car, pulled over maybe five minutes from here, letting the time go by.

She Very clever.

The Husband You didn't dare go any further. You were afraid of meeting up with that man in the road again.

She You see how silly I am, what stupid fears?

The Husband I'm not saying they're stupid.

She Ridiculous.

The Husband Incomprehensible. To be honest, yes. You have to get rid of them.

She You don't know anything at all.

The Husband Damned phone!

She You don't know anything at all.

The Husband Then you explain it.

She There's nothing more to explain.

Pause.

The Husband Do you have to get angry with me?

She I'm not angry with anyone.

The Husband Not even with me.

She Not with anyone.

The Husband Let's just stop for a moment.

She That's what I've been trying to do for some time.

The Husband Look, you see? (*He goes to the telephone, takes it off the hook and leaves it like that.*) There we are.

She Good idea.

He draws near and embraces her again. Mutual passion. Twenty or thirty seconds more. Then **She**, *unexpectedly, moves away from him.*

She No.

The Husband What?

She   It's not helping.

The Husband (*disconcertedly*)   Well, well.

She   I don't want you to touch me.

Silence.

The Husband   What did you say?

She   And I have to go.

The Husband   What did you say?

She   Nothing. Don't look at me like that. Nothing. I'm going now.

The Husband   What do you mean? A minute ago you wanted me near you.

She   I'm going to get your cigarettes.

The Husband   You're planning to go out again?

She   Yes.

The Husband   Why?

She   You need cigarettes.

The Husband   Come on.

She   What?

The Husband   Suddenly you don't want me touching you.

She   Don't confuse things. You know it's not like that.

The Husband   You said I don't know anything.

She   This time . . . This time I'll get there.

The Husband   Oh.

She   I'll drive by the spot where I thought I saw the same man twice. I'll do it. No one will be there and that will be the end of it.

The Husband   All right, but you can wait until tomorrow.

She   Better to sort it out now.

The Husband   Do you want me to go with you?

She   It wouldn't be the same.

The Husband   It's got dark.

She   I'll sort it out now.

She *puts on her coat.*

The Husband   I don't know what to say.

She   It will soon be sorted out.

The Husband   Why did you say you don't want me to touch you?

She *takes the chisel.*

She   Don't worry about that. Words are words. One against the other. They're deceptive, you're right.

The Husband   Don't be too long.

She   I'll see how long it takes.

The Husband   I'll start preparing dinner.

She   All right.

The Husband   What would you like?

She   Whatever you want, you decide.

The Husband   Will you get the cigarettes?

She   I'll try.

The Husband   You said you'd get them.

She   Yes, I said so. Goodbye.

The Husband   Wait!

She   What?

The Husband (*pointing to it*)   The chisel.

She   Do you need it?

The Husband   No, but you're taking it with you.

She   I was aware of that.

The Husband   What do you need it for?

She *does not answer and leaves. Darkness.*

In the darkness, only her face can be seen.

She   Standing dead still and waiting, won't be any use.
Places change with the night.
I'm in the middle of a long, dark, draughty corridor.
I won't be lucky and, if I am, I don't know what I'll do.
I have to defend myself, take revenge.
Too much beer . . . It comes from the beer that sensation of
no and no and no, a no which doesn't stop.
A no which has been dancing around inside me for I don't
know how long.
How long?
I was bad. They used to punish me. There wasn't anything
else they could do.
I used to excite the other children and . . .
Yes, I knew how to play, how to dominate, how to use the
other children.
Those poor women had to punish me, of course.
They used to take me out of a lesson . . .
They used to take me out . . . into the corridor.
Long, in the shadows, solitary, silent.
And the lessons, inside.
I was the one who had chosen the corridor.
Minutes and hours slipped away. In the corridor, nothing.
The years slipped away.
Years and years in the corridor, far away from the class I'd
disturbed.
So, what does it matter now. I'll wait.
In my stomach that no which rises and falls and begins to
grow.

I have to defend myself.
Yes, she has succeeded, but she'll pay for it.
It's her fault everything's become confused.
I won't have any luck, it won't be any use, I won't find her.
First, find her and take revenge; afterwards, I do not know.
He's waiting for me and the cigarettes. Perhaps, then, I
should go back.
And the girls.
They do matter to me.
I lied, I've been lying.
And he realised it. They do matter to me.
He had his mind set on having children.
Now I've got them, and hearing them speak, for example,
hearing them speak . . .
Losing them.
I don't know.
What has happened? What right? How dare they? It
happened.
It doesn't matter, maybe I'll go back.
Still, maybe I'll go back home.
First, I've got to finish this story.
I'd be able to go back if not for the fact that first I've got to
finish it and that I won't finish it, that it's no use my being
here, standing and waiting.
I'd be able to go back if only I could find the way . . . If only
I could find it.
The corridor.
You are very bad. You really did it this time.
It doesn't matter so much. Only a sick mind could . . .
And I paid for it, didn't I?
Oh, yes, I paid the price for it by going out into the
corridor. Years of boredom in the corridor.
Why have you come to look for me?
After years you've come to attack me in the corridor.
Here everything is darkness and silence.
The no and the no and the no. I don't feel well.
The night air . . . I breathe deeply. Perhaps the cold air
will reach my stomach and drown the no and the no and
the no.

In the corridor, often, there was a draught.
The draught, the only thing that would ever come down the
corridor.
But here, apart from the wind, I can hope that, suddenly . . .
Some headlights appear.
The headlights blind me as they round the bend and shine
into my face.
The no and no and no. Anger and disgust.
The headlights filled with a noise that tears through the
night, that floods me with light.
OK. What did they think? Here you have me.
The light comes to a standstill, the noise lowers its pitch.
It was useful, then, to wait in the cold and the confusion.
Here I am. Now what?

V

*A minimal light comes up: it is night. The road, the same place as the
second scene. Her small car, parked to one side, with its headlights on.
In the middle of the road,* **She** *waits. In front of her, the expensive car
has just arrived – it has its engine running and lights her up violently
with its headlights.* **She** *waits, with her coat on, holding the chisel.
The engine of the expensive car stops running.* **The Man** *gets out of
the vehicle. It may not be possible to distinguish the silhouette of another
person who is still inside.*

She   Now what?

The Man   Have you got a problem?

She   Yes.

The Man   Can I help you?

She   My car . . . (**She** *cannot find the words.*)

The Man   It's broken down in the night and in the middle
of nowhere.

She   Yes.

The Man   We'll fix it, don't worry.

She   I need someone to . . . (**She** *cannot find the words.*)

The Man (*encouraging her*)   Yes, me.

She   Someone to take me, to take me to a service garage.

The Man   Of course.

She   Do you know what time it is?

The Man   Let me look at my watch.

She   It's late. Late. The service garages are closed. Hadn't you realised?

The Man   We'll find somewhere else, no need to worry.

She   I see you've fixed it . . . Your . . . your one.

The Man   Mine?

She   It must have been just a minor problem.

The Man   My car?

She   You were lucky.

The Man   It hasn't been fixed. Not today, at least.

She   Hasn't it?

The Man   I had it checked a month ago. Do you mean a breakdown?

She   The breakdown this afternoon.

The Man   Luckily it's been a while since I've had one.

She   That's odd. Now I'm having the same difficulties.

The Man   Sorry?

She   What should we do?

The Man   Get going, don't you think? We should get going. You must be freezing.

She   I've got my coat on. I didn't know if you'd drive by here, I didn't know how long, how many hours I'd have to wait.

The Man   Leave it to me. How do you prefer us to do this?

She   At the same spot in the road. Exactly the same spot where I picked you up this afternoon.

The Man   Sorry?

She   Now you'll be the one to pick *me* up. Incredible.

The Man   Excuse me, I don't follow you.

She   Do you feel the same shame that I feel?

The Man   My dear woman . . .

She   In any case you could have driven past. No, I knew that if we were going to meet again you wouldn't drive past.

The Man   Meet again?

She (*as her anger begins to increase*)   Oh, no, no way!

The Man   Where did we meet up?

She   Would you dare? I took you to the cafeteria and you made me go through a pitiful scene there . . . Would you like to forget about that, too, blot it out, deny it?

The Man   My dear woman, I don't know what you're talking about.

She   Why am I here then?

The Man   Well, your car had a breakdown.

She   Yes, my car, just fancy that, had a breakdown.

The Man   I'd be pleased to . . .

She   How do you do it?

The Man   I'll help you. I'd be pleased to.

She   How do you do it?

The Man   It's not as if I've got much time. If you don't mind, we should get going.

She (*drily*)   Have some patience.

The Man   Fine, whatever's needed.

She   What shall we do?

The Man   Didn't you ask me how I do it? I don't have much time. That helps me to know how to do it. It also helps me to know how to have patience.

She   Bastard!

The Man   Why are you insulting me?

She   Yes, I've insulted you, go away. Will you still help a woman who's insulting you? Go away!

The Man   You need help. I can't leave you here alone.

She   And if I attacked you?

The Man   Why would you attack me?

She   Don't you know me? Haven't you ever seen me before? You don't know me, I speak to you the way I'm speaking to you, and you don't get angry, you don't fire off at me, you refuse to put an end to your slimy pleasantries . . .

The Man   Calm down.

She   I know what's going on.

The Man   We should sort out the breakdown of your vehicle. And leave you in a safe place.

She (*laughing*)   Which safe place?

The Man   Wherever you want.

She   Which safe place?

Pause.

The Man   Will you allow me?

She   What?

The Man   Perhaps you think I'm being too cheeky.

She   What do you want now?

The Man   Don't get angry.

She   What do you want?

The Man   I see you're . . . It's a stupid assumption, of course.

She   What do you see?

The Man   You're frightened.

She   Frightened?

The Man   Sorry, I shouldn't say such things.

She   I am not frightened.

The Man   I was wrong, that's not the right word.

She   I'm not, don't get your hopes up.

The Man   I tend to express myself badly.

She   In any case, I'm not.

The Man   But if you were . . .

She   I'm not.

The Man   But if inside you there was . . . Please understand, it's a childish pretension, I know. If inside you . . . I mean, if inside you there was still the shadow of a concern that I have no reason to know about, which, of course, has nothing to do with me . . . A concern which is not a fear but which, forgive me, is sort of like a fear . . .; in that hypothetical . . . and absurd case . . .

She   Completely absurd.

The Man   In that case, that's not it and I have no reason
to bring it up . . .

She   What?

The Man   In that case I'd like – you see how ridiculous it
is – I'd like to tell you, I'll only take a minute of your time,
about a story I remember from when I was young.

She   Oh, really?

The Man   Just a minute.

She   A story from when you were young? Now? Here?

The Man   If you'd allow me.

She   Standing out here in the cold, and you want to tell
me what you used to do when you were young.

The Man   A little anecdote.

She   My God!

The Man   Don't take it the wrong way. Perhaps it'll help
you.

She   In what way? How?

The Man   Perhaps it'll help you.

Pause.

She   Hurry up.

The Man   Right. I was young, a child. A frightened child
in unpleasant times. One night, after dinner, well, as always,
they put me to bed and, I don't remember, I suppose I fell
asleep. But, suddenly, and it was strange, normally, like all
children, I was used to falling asleep straight away, suddenly
I woke up again. Everything was completely dark. I had the
feeling, I suppose I interpreted it in a different way, the
feeling that I had fallen into the heart of the night. And
some faint sounds could be heard. Furtive, constant sounds.
Someone was moving, someone was watching me and, you
can imagine, probably would have pounced on me, and so

on. I didn't dare scream or move. A kind of absolute terror, poor child. A long while passed, at least it seemed like it. The faint sounds didn't stop, the whispering, the rustling. They were laughing at me, prolonging the torture before the final attack. I couldn't take it any more and then . . . Why wait? Why not throw myself over the edge and end it once and for all? I got up, I stepped forward through the darkness, I bumped into a door . . . I opened it and left the evil behind. And that's how I surprised my parents, who were putting together a surprise present for me, for my birthday. It was the best birthday of my life.

She   Finished?

The Man   It isn't an original story, everyone has lived through a similar experience.

She   Why did you tell it to me? What's it to me?

The Man   Actually, I don't know.

She   I've had enough.

The Man   Come on. Give me your car keys.

She   Why do you need them? Shouldn't I be going with you?

The Man   There's no need.

She   And what will I do?

The Man   Stay.

She   Where?

The Man   My car is comfortable.

She   Weren't you going to leave me in a safe place.

The Man   My car is a completely safe place.

She   We both know what's going on.

The Man   Will you give me the keys?

She   Isn't it dangerous, for you?

The Man   For me? I'm ill, I've got very little time left and she doesn't know. What danger could there be?

She   I'm sorry.

The Man   I'm sorry for what I've put you through.

She *hands the keys over to him.*

She   Just go, will you.

The Man   Yes, it's time to put an end to this. Good night. (*He breathes deeply.*) Oh it is a good night, after all, isn't it?

She   Rain, cold and wind.

The Man   A very good night.

He gets into her small car, closes the door, starts it up in a completely normal way, and sets off. He and the vehicle disappear. **She** *watches him go. The sound of the car becomes more distant, diminishes, fades away. Then* **She** *turns round again to face the headlights that blind her. Pause.* **The Woman** *gets out of the expensive car. Standing, separated by a certain distance, they stare at each other.*

She (*without surprise, after a moment*)   What do you want? Why have you come, again? You were wrong to come. Why do you think I've come? Now maybe you'll leave me alone. I don't feel sorry for you and I'm not afraid of you either. I'll make you leave me alone. By force, if necessary. (*Pause.*) What right do you think you have? What are you looking for? Now, at this point in time, what? You won't get away with it. (**The Woman** *holds an arm out to her, with the palm of her hand open.*) No! (**She** *steps back, startled.* **The Woman** *keeps her arm held out.*) Go away! Leave me alone! Go away! (*Long pause. Then* **She** *moves forward, lifts the chisel and drops it on the outstretched arm.* **The Woman** *withdraws her arm and her whole body.* **She** *remains paralysed.* **She** *lets the weapon fall to the ground.*) It's one of my husband's tools. Now I won't be able to give it back to him. (**She** *raises a hand to her mouth and another to her stomach, runs off within reach of the glare of the headlights and practically disappears; we hear her vomit.* **The Woman** *takes out a white handkerchief and places it on the wound on her arm.* **She** *comes* *back.* **She** *looks at* **The Woman**. *Naturally*.) I had a lot to drink. (**The Woman** *takes away the handkerchief, looks at a stain made by the blood, and immediately brings the same stained handkerchief to the other's lips, wiping them.* **She** *lets* **The Woman** *do it. Pause.*) The cupboard, the clock and the quilt.

Fourplay

by

Sergi Belbel

translated by

Sharon G. Feldman

To J.R.

Premiere in Catalan
Teatre Romea, Barcelona, 19 April 1990, directed by Sergi
Belbel.

Premiere Production of the English translation
Lyric Studio Hammersmith, London, 2 February 1999,
directed by Hans-Peter Kellner; designed by Simon D.
Beresford.

The Man	Mark A. Benson
The Woman	Joscelyn Best
The Male Friend	Scott Maslen
The Female Friend	Debra Tammer

Characters

The Man
The Woman
The Male Friend
The Female Friend

Place
A completely empty bedroom, without doors or windows,
with an enormous bed (two by two metres), off-centre to the
right.

Time
– Real: from approximately three in the afternoon to nine in
the morning on the following day. Any day.
– Within the individual scenes: odd-numbered scenes
advance forward in time, even-numbered scenes go
backwards.

Structure
– First part: nineteen brief sequences, separated by
darkness (scenes one to nineteen).
– Second part: one single scene composed of nineteen
sequences, with scene changes visible to the audience (scenes
twenty to thirty-eight).

Scene One

An empty bedroom without the bed. Voices of **The Man** *and* **The Woman**.

The Woman   What then?

The Man   What?

The Woman   That's right, what?

The Man   What what?

The Woman   When will it be here, then?

The Man   When will it be here?

The Woman   Yes, when will it be here, then.

Pause.

The Man   Now, right now.

The Woman   Right now?

The Man   Right now.

Pause.

The Woman   Are you sure?

The Man   I'm sure.

Pause.

The Woman   I hope this isn't another one of your awful little jokes?

The Man   How dare you say that? A joke? How could it possibly be a joke, when we've been planning it for months?

The Woman   You mean, *you*'ve been planning it for months.

The Man   All right, let's be honest, for a change: *I*'ve been planning it for months. Yes, me, just me.

The Woman   Hold on a minute! *I*'ve done my bit, as well!

The Man Hold on a minute! *You*'ve done your bit, as well!

The Woman   I was the one who suggested more more more more . . . space.

The Man   Comfort.

The Woman   Space.

The Man   Ease.

The Woman   Space, space.

The Man   I mean: comfort, ease. In a word, freedom.

The Woman   Sometimes you say the strangest things . . .

Pause.

The Man   What things?

Pause.

The Woman   Are you sure it will be here today? This afternoon? In a little while? Right now, as you said? So, may I may I may I may I may I go and get them?

The Man   Get them?

The Woman   You know perfectly well I ordered them over a month ago. Oh, I made them promise they would have them ready for me in two weeks. And I swore I would go and pick them up two weeks ago, thinking, of course, that two weeks ago it would already have been here.

The Man   Oh, right. I didn't realise what you were talking about.

The Woman   Well, that's it, I'm going to get them.

The Man   Aren't you going to wait for it to come?

Woman You mean: for them to bring it?

The Man   For them to bring it?

The Woman   Well, it's certainly not going to come by itself, is it?

Pause.

The Man Of course not.

The Woman You did say right now? Right now, yes? Right now? Well, it's already been 'right now' for the past two hours, hasn't it?, and 'right now' is already now, if I'm not mistaken, and it still hasn't come, it hasn't come, it hasn't come; at least, as far as I can see I can't see anything here, here, anything at all, anything at all, anything at all, oh oh oh we're going to end up without anything, tonight, tonight we'll have to sleep on the street if we go on like this, two hours like two idiots since they took the other one away, and there's still no sign of the new one, is there? Oh, yes, yes, yes, I'm going I'm going I'm going, perhaps we'll be lucky but I'm still going, perhaps if I leave, your 'right now right now' will become a reality and, then!, what a stroke of luck and it comes at that very instant; now if that happens, it's not a good sign!, it will mean that it doesn't like me! I'm going. I'll die of embarrassment when they see me walk in. Two weeks late! The way I hurried them to to to to put it together (oh, is that how you say it?, put it together?). And what, well, then, you, what do you think?, shall I go? is it clear to you or or or or not, come on, what do you think?

The Man Goodbye.

The Woman Oh.

The Man Yes, yes, yes, you'd better go. Better. Better. Better.

The Woman Well, then, now it's definite: I'm going.

The Man I'm sure that . . .

The Woman That what?

Pause.

The Woman If you need anything . . .

The Man Hmm . . . At the moment, I don't know.

The Woman   Well, then, goodbye.

The Man   Wait.

The Woman   What?

The Man   Will you be long?

The Woman   Well, look, I don't know. I've got to go quite a long way. I may be.

The Man   Oh, so I don't think that . . .

The Woman   That what?

The Man   Are you sure you don't want . . . You prefer . . . ?

The Woman   It's just that I can't stay here any longer. I'm tired of doing nothing and I'm going to go and do what I should have done some time ago. I'm feeling very restless and stressed out, you know, so you stay here by yourself and I'll go. It'll be all right, in fact, just the opposite, it'll be better, because I know that . . .

The Man   Do you want me to go . . .

The Woman   No, no, no, no. You can't leave. You have to stay put. Just imagine if . . . Besides besides, I can do it by myself. By myself I can.

The Man   You mean?

The Woman   Of course! Of course, I can, you'll see, I don't think I'll get too tired, no, I don't think I'll get too tired, don't worry about me.

The Man   Fine, do what you want.

The Woman   Right. Come on then, that's enough pointless chattering away, as always. So . . . goodbye. Goodbye. Goodbye. Goodbye.

Darkness.

Scene Two

Lights. **The Man**, **The Woman**, **The Male Friend** *and* **The Female Friend**, *each of them seated at one of the corners of the bed.* **The Male Friend** *and* **The Female Friend** *in sensual positions.* **The Man**, *smiling,* **The Woman**, *excited.*

The Male Friend   I've got to go.

The Female Friend   I've got to go.

The Male Friend   I have to go to work.

The Female Friend   Me too. To work.

The Male Friend   I'm so tired.

The Female Friend   My back aches. It aches right here, in my spine . . . Oh, it feels as if I . . . as if I'd . . .

The Woman   As if you'd nothing, love. Nothing at all. Everything is just as it was . . .

The Female Friend   I'm going.

The Male Friend   Me too.

The Woman   Me too.

The Man   What?

Pause.

The Woman   I'm going.

The Man   Where?

The Woman   I mean I'm leaving, I mean I'm not going anywhere in particular, no, no, I mean I'm going away, in . . . in general, I mean . . . not at all. Everything has turned out so terribly . . .

The Female Friend *gets up, walks in front of* **The Man** *and* **The Woman**, *and goes towards* **The Male Friend**. *She holds out her hand to him.*

The Female Friend   Well, it's been a pleasure, a pleasure to meet you, I really have had an evening . . . a very . . . I mean, a night . . . really, it's been years and years and years and years since I've had, I can assure you, believe me.

The Male Friend   Yes, yes, me, too. I mean . . . me neither.

The Male Friend *coughs.* **The Female Friend** *points to his trouser pocket. He puts his hand in and takes out three extinguished cigarette butts.*

Male Friend   Of course, too much smoke.

The Female Friend   Right.

The Male Friend *gets up.*

The Male Friend   Goodbye.

The Female Friend   Goodbye.

The Man *looks at* **The Woman**.

The Man   Goodbye, then.

Darkness.

Scene Three

Lights. **The Man**, *by himself, stares at the bed from a distance.*

The Man   Yes. Yes. Yes. Here we have it, our two-by-two, at last. Fantastic. Just right. That's it, just right. That's it. Or perhaps . . .

He goes up to the bed.

But no. No.

Pause.

A TWO-BY-TWO.

Pause.

Sorry? What? Excuse me? Oh, yes, yes: the advantages of a two-by-two metre bed?: ALL OF THEM, to put it in a deliberately simplistic way.

Pause.

In the first place, I should mention the numerical coincidence before going into detail: a two-by-two for two. To put it another way: a bed for two because there are two. Yes, that's it. There are two . . . bodies. In this case, mine and her her her hers. I mean: a single body for two bodies. Man and woman, masculine and feminine, duality that doesn't necessarily overstate itself but that implicitly conveys an inanimate object, asexual, not modulated of course, not stratified that is the beeeed. Or as well: my . . . our two-by-two bed, double bed, for two, whose essence lies in its measurements, and whose only function lies in the utopian union for the nocturnal repose of two individuals of the opposite sex. Yes. Of the opposite sex. Of the opposite . . . sex. Sex . . . opposite. Yes. Opposite . . . sex.

Pause.

So, the first conclusion, the result of a simple mathematical operation – division – or bearing in mind, just, the parametric co-ordinates pertaining to a purely formal and objective delimitation and leaving aside any connotative implication that could invite misunderstandings of a subjective nature – in other words, everything immersed in an affective level which, because of its very nature, transgresses the merely denotative environment (which is the one that interests me, to begin with) – is, logically, the following:

Pause.

. . . two metres . . . two bodies . . . A METRE FOR EACH BODY!

Pause. He appears satisfied with his conclusions.

In other words: one body for each metre. Or a single body
in each one of the metres. Or just one body – be it male or
female, mine or that . . . which is hers – in each one of the
half-spaces, right or left, so dividing, a single metre! One for
me and one for her, two spaces in the two-by-two, one for
oneself and one not, one definitely mine and the other
someone else's, the other: hers, and the two of us the same
size in this SINGLE and unique object (entire nights and
nights and nights designing it) which I know is completely
indivisible.

Pause.

Of course, since she . . . I mean, since I . . . she and I in the
one we had before we . . . there wasn't . . . That is to say, of
course, the one we had before . . . and she would always . . .
well, oh, right?, oh!, well, she, well, hey, she's still not back,
she's still not back?, no she's still not back, a long way, yes,
yes, she must have gone quite a long way because she's still
not back, and will she bring them?, will she bring them?, or
won't she bring them?

A scream from **The Woman**. **The Man** *becomes frightened.*

Voice of The Woman   Oh! Oh! Oh! Has it finally
come?!

The Man   Yes!

Voice of The Woman   Oh, this is heavy, heavy, heavy, I
can't, help, help!

The Man   She's brought them.

Darkness.

Scene Four

Lights. **The Male Friend** *and* **The Female Friend**. *On the
floor, two extinguished cigarette butts.* **The Female Friend**,
wearing only a night shirt and knickers, is finishing a cigarette.

The Female Friend   Hmm . . . a slight problem, just a slight problem: if you are you and I am me, and the bed is a bed (above all the bed, of course, which is a bed and nothing more, as I already know very well thanks to you), so, here, in my opinion, this place where we are right now, should be a BEDROOM AND NOT AN ASHTRAY!!!

Quickly, **The Male Friend** *picks up the cigarette butts from the floor and blows on the ashes.* **The Female Friend** *looks at him and, ceremoniously, puts out her cigarette on her shoe and offers the butt to him.*

Female Friend   A present.

The Male Friend   Thank you.

The Female Friend   Don't mention it.

The Female Friend *places the extinguished cigarette in* **The Male Friend**'s *outstretched hand, next to the others. Both of them remain silent, staring at the cigarette butts.*

The Male Friend/The Female Friend   What a stench!

The Male Friend   Sorry?

The Female Friend   What?

Darkness.

Scene Five

Darkness. Someone is heard energetically clapping their hands. Lights. **The Man** *and* **The Woman**. *In the centre of the bedroom, a parcel. It was* **The Woman** *who was clapping, in ecstasy, and admiring the bed from a distance.* **The Man**, *unmoved, gestures to her to stop clapping.* **The Woman** *calms down and gives him an apologetic look.* **The Man** *measures the right side of the bed, centimetre by centimetre. Meanwhile,* **The Woman** *mumbles in a low voice. When he finishes, he looks at* **The Woman** *and gives her* *a nod of approval.* **The Woman** *smiles. The same thing with the lower side. The same with the left side. The same with the upper side.*

Pause.

The Man *straightens up and moves away from the bed.* **The Woman** *calms down and makes a grand gesture as though she were going to fling herself on top of the bed.* **The Man** *stops her with a severe and concise gesture.* **The Woman** *remains rooted to the spot and looks at him questioningly ('why not?').* **The Man** *answers her with a vague gesture ('not yet').* **The Woman** *sits up.* **The Man** *goes up to the bed.* **The Woman** *moves away from it.* **The Man** *moves around the bed, measuring it, counting his steps in a low voice. Gestures of approval.* **The Woman** *claps with joy. Gesture from* **The Man** *telling her not to make any noise (he needs to concentrate).* **The Man** *moves away from the bed.* **The Woman** *goes up to the bed and, once again, looks as though she is about to hurl herself on top of it. Gesture from* **The Man** *to prevent her from trying to jump again. Gestures from* **The Woman** *to calm him down ('I wasn't planning on doing it, oh, you're such a pain'). Gesture from* **The Woman** *asking him to let her touch the bed. Gesture from* **The Man** *('not yet'). Gesture from* **The Woman** *('not even a little bit?'). Gesture from* **The Man** *('no!'). Gesture from* **The Woman** *('just a little bit?'). Gesture from* **The Man** *('I said "no!"').*

Pause.

The Woman   Why not?

The Man   Because you can't.

The Woman   Oh. It's fragile.

The Man   No. It's strong.

The Woman   Oh.

Pause.

The Woman   Who put it here?

The Man   Me.

The Woman   You?

The Man   Me.

The Woman   All by yourself?

The Man   All by myself.

The Woman   Could you manage?

The Man   I could.

The Woman   It's not heavy?

The Man   It's not heavy.

The Woman   AAAHHH! OHHH!! It's not heavy! It's not heavy, it's not heavy!! How marvellous! It's not heavy. We'll put it here, we'll put it there, like that or like that, to the right and turned round, and so on!

Pause.

The Man   If you remember, we agreed that it was important for it to be simple, light, agile, light, dynamic and light, forgoing all complications and extravagances. Light, yes, light, but solid, too. In its own way. And here it is, just like that. I'm quite pleased with it. I like the way it turned out.

The Woman   Are you sure about it?

The Man   Yes.

The Woman   Convinced?

The Man   Yes.

The Woman   Yes?

The Man   Yes.

Pause. **The Woman** *points at the parcel and looks at* **The Man**.

The Woman   May I?

Darkness.

Scene Six

Lights. **The Male Friend**, *by himself, sings: 'Strangers in the Night'.*

Darkness.

Scene Seven

Darkness. Noise of paper that someone is tearing and crumpling up. Lights. Some patterned fabric waving in the air. Bits of paper on the floor. **The Woman**, *under the fabric (sheets). She lets out a rather hysterical scream when she finds that she cannot get out from under them (she opened the parcel and took them out in such a rush that she has become entangled in them). Finally, she manages to free herself from the sheets and throws them on the bed. She exhales and fixes her hair. Nervous, excited, she moves towards the bed. In a great hurry (she is really anxious about seeing the bed all made up and neat), she separates the sheets (the bottom and the top sheet). She stretches out the bottom sheet and covers the bed with it. She stretches out the top sheet. She quickly moves away from the bed to the other side of the room in order to see what it looks like.*

Pause.

The bed, frankly, is poorly made up: wrinkles all around, corners that hang, uneven on all sides, etc.

The Woman   Oh, oh, oh!, what a mess and what a disaster, oh, how awful, how awful!

In a fit of fury and shame she moves towards the bed, tears off the sheets and throws them on the floor. Pause. She calms down. She exhales. She looks at the bed. She looks at the sheets. She seems to be in deep concentration.

The Woman   A second time, a second time, everything always turns out great the second time round. Now, come on, let's try again. Without rushing this time.

Smiling, she grabs the bottom sheet and unfurls it in the air. She lets it fall gently on the bed. With great care, with very delicate gestures, she takes the top sheet and places it gracefully on the bed. She evens out the wrinkles, checks that the corners and the ends etc. are the same. While she does all this, she sings a parody of 'My Way'.

Pause. She moves away from the bed and looks at it all. She smiles with satisfaction.

Oh. How stunning! Now that's it.

Pause.

That's it.

Darkness.

Scene Eight

Lights. **The Male Friend** *and* **The Female Friend**. **The Male Friend** *is sitting on the floor, with a lost look, calmly smoking a cigarette.* **The Female Friend**, *standing, at the side of the bed, wearing only her knickers, bra and high-heeled shoes, lets out a cry of desperation and obsessively examines her hands.*

The Female Friend   Aaaaah!!

Pause.

Help me. Help me. Help me. Help me. I can't, can't you see?, I can't do it, there's a resistance, a contrary force, reactionary, contrary to the impulse, to the natural impulse, to the impulse I have, that comes from inside me, and it's preventing me, you see, oh, what shit!, you saw, how embarrassing, you saw, didn't you?, or no, or perhaps not?, but, so, the thing is there's no way, it won't open, it doesn't want to, yes, yes, that's it, it's the one who doesn't want to, oh, not me!, it's not me, you saw, didn't you?, oh, it doesn't want to, it won't let me, it's keeping me from, what?, oh!, bloody reactionary thing!, and it's also the fault of the fucking, this fucking thing in the back, yes, that's it, it's the one, and it's also this other thing, it's their fault!

Darkness.

Scene Nine

Lights. **The Man** *and* **The Woman**.

The Woman   I don't know if I should cry.

The Man   Don't take it that way.

The Woman   I do take it that way . . . and more.

Pause.

The Woman   I think I'm going to cry.

The Man   It's nothing to cry about.

The Woman   It is something to cry about . . . and more.

Pause.

The Woman   It takes very little. Very little.

The Man   For what?

The Woman   For me to cry.

The Man   We shouldn't attach so much importance to it.

The Woman   We should attach so much importance to it
. . . and more.

Pause.

The Woman   I'm crying.

The Man   Crying won't solve anything.

The Woman   Then, well, I'll stop crying because this
problem has to be solved some way or another.

Pause.

The Woman   I've stopped crying.

The Man   That sounds fine to me. Now what?

The Woman   I think I want to be alone, to think things over.

Pause.

The Woman   I knew it.

The Man   What?

The Woman   That.

Pause.

The Woman   I've got a theory.

Pause.

The Man   About what?

The Woman   About what's happening.

Pause.

The Man   Tell me.

The Woman   Do you know who's to blame?

The Man   For what?

The Woman   For what's just happened to us.

The Man   No. Who?

The Woman   I don't know if I should tell you.

The Man   Why?

The Woman   Because I know you'll laugh.

The Man   I won't laugh.

The Woman   You will laugh.

The Man   Whose fault is it? Mine?

The Woman   No. Not yours.

The Man   Whose is it, then?

The Woman   It's . . .

Darkness.

Scene Ten

Lights. **The Female Friend***, by herself, facing the audience. She smiles maliciously.*

The Female Friend   Yes, much more . . . much more . . . Yes, yes, yes, this is my great opportunity!

She adopts a provocative pose. She sticks out her tongue.

Yoo hoo!

She struts about in a sensual way, looking at the audience.

Good evening . . .

She stops. She comes out of the pose.

Oh, no, no, even better!

With a high level of eroticism, she does a striptease, like a cabaret performer, until she is standing in her bra and knickers. She looks at the audience.

Hello, how're you doing?

Darkness.

Scene Eleven

Lights. **The Woman***, by herself, moving around the bed in circles.*

The Woman   I don't understand anything at all.

Pause.

Why? Why? Why?

Pause.

And how?

Pause.

Oh. Make fun of it. Make fun of it. But how can I make fun of it?

Pause. She looks at the bed.

Oh, it's already making me nervous, yes, it's making me hysterical, hysterical! It's beginning to make me hysterical, this thing! Ugh! Not good. If it's already making me nervous now, oh, how awful! All new, so new, too new!

Pause.

Make fun of it . . . Make fun of it . . . But how can I make fun of ill-fated Destiny? Destiny! Oh, fucking destiny! Fucking bed! And fucking sheets! Fucking evening and all that time wasted! Oh, yes, fucking everything!!

She starts to make a gesture of furious rage towards the bed, but then she restrains herself, amusingly.

Darkness.

Scene Twelve

Lights. **The Male Friend**, *by himself, in the centre of the bedroom, facing the audience. He has one hand in his trouser pocket. He shakes, somewhat obscenely, the inside of his pocket. He takes out his hand. He moves his fingers as if there were something 'stuck' to them. He smells his fingers. He looks at them. He smells them again. He loves the smell.*

The Male Friend   Oh. What a stench. Mouldy.

Pause. He lets his gaze wander about the bedroom until he sees the bed.

Fantastic.

Pause. He looks at his body, his hands.

Not sweets.

Pause.

Or flowers.

Pause.

Or champagne, either.

Pause.

I'm a man of my time.

Pause. He looks at the bed.

Like you.

Darkness.

Scene Thirteen

Lights. **The Man** *and* **The Woman**. **The Woman** *slaps* **The Man** *violently*.

The Woman   Your sweet revenge, eh? You did it on purpose, didn't you?

The Man   No.

The Woman   Well, it seemed that way to me, all the signs were there.

The Man   You're right, I did it on purpose, but it was for your own good, to fix it for you, that's the way it's done, believe me, with one swift blow. Try it and you'll see.

The Woman *takes a few steps.*

The Man   Better?

The Woman   Better.

The Man   You see?

The Woman   Thank you and I'm sorry.

Pause.

The Woman   Well, let's get on with it: you take care of him and I'll take care of her. It's obvious.

The Man   It makes sense.

The Woman   It's normal and don't interrupt me. Now, well, by phone, just a date. No explanations on the phone. I hate the phone. And even more so today, of course, after those pitiful calls. Oh, don't remind me of them.

The Man   I didn't remind you of anything.

The Woman   Be quiet and don't make me lose my concentration! Yes, that's it, ring them up straight away. And then . . .

The Man   What?

The Woman   Shut up! . . .

The Man   Sorry.

The Woman   Then . . . they arrive, they see, and we attack.

The Man   OK.

The Woman   You take him.

The Man   And you take her.

They look at each other.

Darkness.

Scene Fourteen

Lights. **The Man**, **The Woman** *and* **The Female Friend**. **The Man** *is crouching at the side of the bed, meticulously examining one of its corners. On the other side,* **The Female Friend**, *radiant with joy, walks towards* **The Woman** *with open arms. All of a sudden, she makes a funny and exaggerated leap, as in a circus act.*

The Woman *lets out a wild shriek, also smiling.* **The Female Friend** *lets herself fall spectacularly on the floor, on her back.* **The Woman** *goes up to* **The Female Friend**, *opens her legs like a ballerina, and also lets herself drop to the ground.* **The Female Friend** *screams and gets up.* **The Woman** *stretches out her hand to her so that* **The Female Friend** *can stand up.* **The Female Friend** *gives her her hand and both of them outline, between exclamations of joy, a strange choreographed spectacle. Finally,* **The Woman** *pulls* **The Female Friend** *energetically, who falls brusquely on her. Simultaneous squeals from both of them.* **The Man** *does not seem to have noticed anything that is going on. Pause.*

The Man   I think something's cracked.

Darkness.

Scene Fifteen

Lights. **The Man** *and* **The Male Friend**. *Both facing the audience.* **The Man** *grabs* **The Male Friend** *by the shoulders, preventing him from turning to see the bed.*

The Male Friend   What's that there behind us, my friend?

The Man   Not yet.

The Male Friend   You like mysteries. I like mysteries. I like mysterious encounters, they excite me. I haven't played hard to get. I didn't take long to get here. I've come. And now you won't let me see.

The Man   Not yet.

The Male Friend   I'm almost trembling with expectation.

The Man   Not yet, not yet.

Pause.

The Male Friend   Speak!

Pause.

The Man   It's special, very special. Dimensions that may seem implausible to you (nevertheless, they're well calculated). I myself am the designer: two by two metres. Someday I'll explain why. When I finally figure it out. I still don't know. Notice notice notice the spatial layout. Spatial here means 'in space'. Its position. It's very important, too important for someone like you not to notice, when it comes to formulating, postulating, formulating a judgement (I know you'll inevitably do it, I know you too well). Just right. Balanced in a logic of disequilibrium. I'll go on. It's just that I'd prefer to prepare you for it, to warn you.

The Male Friend   I like listening to you.

The Man   The Dimensions. The Position. Thirdly: the Material. Noble. Noble. Noble. Like me, like you, discreet and masculine. To sum up, a noble material. Dimensions. Position. Material. After that: Character. The most difficult, the character, the design of the character. What made my head spin night after night (I couldn't sleep). Sober, sober, sobriety, above all, sobriety, sensible sobriety and sensible above all. Overwhelming blow from the edges, rotund firmness of the corners, predictable autonomy, vigorous simplicity, visible functionality, energetic receipt of repose, maximum resistance at the limit of the wildest coitus, and above all: material mutability (I can't stand carelessness!). That's it, its character.

The Male Friend   Oh. Don't stop, don't stop.

The Man   And finally: Action. Action, which is a condition. Action inherent in the character (I just told you about that), required by the dimensional and material contents, although still to be resolved. (I don't know if you understand me.) It's the invitation: the rhythmic and zigzagging convulsions of the pre-orgiastic act that has yet to be consummated. The unrepeatable moment, which humbly and generously I've wanted to offer you. I don't know if you understand me but that's why you're here!

The Male Friend   Ah!

The Man   Now you're prepared. Now you are. You're in an optimum condition to judge and admire it, look at it and criticise it, my dear friend. Remember: Dimensions, Position, Material, Character, and Action and/or Condition.

Pause.

The Man   You can turn round.

The Man *lets go of him.* **The Male Friend** *turns round. Silence.*

The Male Friend   Oh!

Pause.

The Male Friend   I'm speechless.

The Man   You don't need to say anything.

The Male Friend   Oh!

The Male Friend *cries.*

The Man   You're crying.

The Male Friend   Tears of joy. I'm so moved.

The Man   You make me so happy.

The Male Friend   You're a genius, you're a genius, you're a genius, kiss me, my friend, my head is spinning, come, come and give me a hug, my friend, I need you to touch me, grab me, take me in your arms . . .

Darkness.

Scene Sixteen

Lights. **The Woman** *and* **The Female Friend** *on either side of the bed.*

The Female Friend   No.

The Woman *looks at* **The Female Friend**. *Pause.* **The Woman** *goes up to* **The Female Friend**.

The Woman   You've been looking rather thin lately. You can't have been eating properly, I can tell from the colour of your face. Have you looked at yourself in the mirror lately? Your skin is drier than ever and your cheekbones look awfully prominent, jutting out. Deep wrinkles are visible at the corners of your eyes, and you've already got dark rings under them like bin-bags. Have you been to the doctor? You've got to, got to, got to go, please, in case you're suffering from something serious. Extremely serious. Oh, look at you!, look at you, you've got some kind of yellow scaly thing underneath your lips, on your chin, and you have all that chafing on your neck! Malnutrition? Exhaustion? Stress? Anxiety? . . . No, I know what it is: neglect! Oh, I don't believe it. Ugh!, and that hair?! You look absolutely terrible. We'll have to do something about this, because if we don't . . .

The Female Friend   You know what?, I hadn't even noticed, I hadn't even noticed.

Darkness.

Scene Seventeen

Lights. **The Woman**, **The Man**, *and* **The Male Friend**. *All three, motionless, forming a semicircle facing the audience, stare at a part of the floor.*

The Woman   And that?

The Man   That?

The Woman   Yes: that.

The Male Friend   I . . .

The Man   The Stendhal syndrome.

The Male Friend   The Stendhal syndrome, that's right.

The Woman   Oh.

Pause.

The Woman   And?

The Man   What?

The Woman   The thing.

The Man   The thing?

The Woman   Not yet . . . ?

The Man   Not . . . what?

The Woman   You haven't . . . ? You haven't yet . . . ?

The Man   Oh. Yes, yes . . . I was going to, I was going to, but you see.

The Woman   Yes, I see.

The Male Friend   If I'm bothering you . . .

Pause.

The Woman   Well, as you probably already know, the thing refers to what they just brought us.

The Male Friend   Oh.

The Woman   The thing refers to tonight, as you well know.

The Male Friend   Oh.

The Woman   And since you know perfectly well that the thing is that he and I, we can't . . .

The Male Friend   Oh.

The Woman   . . . You also probably know that it upsets us not to be able to.

The Male Friend   Yes, of course . . .

The Woman   And I thought (this, too, you probably know): 'so new, new, and with this smell of newness, will it stay that way until tomorrow? OH, NO!'

The Male Friend   Oh.

Pause.

The Man   Do you understand?

The Male Friend   Eh?

The Man   She said: 'OH, NO!'

The Male Friend   Oh.

The Man   'OH, NO!'

The Male Friend   Yes.

The Man   Yes, no: NO!

The Woman   No.

The Male Friend   No, no, of course.

Pause.

The Woman   To think that I even cried!

The Male Friend   Oh.

The Woman   Out of anger!

The Man   You must understand what's worrying us.

The Male Friend   Yes, yes.

The Woman   That's why you're here, you know.

The Male Friend   That?

The Man   Yes, yes, remember: 'action inherent in the character' . . .

The Male Friend   Oh.

Pause.

The Woman What the hell did you say, if you don't mind?

Pause.

The Man I understand your silence. You need to think about it.

The Male Friend Hmm . . . yes.

The Man Think it over slowly, of course.

The Male Friend Of course.

The Man Are you having doubts?

The Male Friend Well . . . what do you expect me to say?

The Woman A man like you, so young and vigorous and adventurous, can never say no.

The Male Friend Hmm . . . of course . . . not.

The Man So, you accept?

Pause.

The Male Friend The truth is that . . . that . . .

Pause. **The Woman** *stares at* **The Man** *and gives him a strong slap on the back.*

The Woman Listen, dear, I'm under the impression that either this bloke hasn't understood anything at all or he just doesn't know anything about it. Now, what doesn't surprise me at all is that, probably all this while, instead of telling him what you had to tell him, you've been chatting about the hibernation of mussels in the North Pole, about the orthogonal bisectors of Aristotelian philosophy or about the 'actions inherent in crepuscular characters' . . . No, no, that's fine by me, you know?, it's perfectly fine by me, really, I like to gossip, too, I think it feeds the soul, you know?, but of course, it just so happens that he's here, among other things, for this thing, which of course is my idea, therefore,

if he is here it is thanks to me, and, of course, I don't mind if
you waste saliva on your concept of a 'sub-realist' aesthetic,
of course not!, on the other hand there are some things
which really get me going, you know?, that really turn me
on, you know?, what I mean is, I do it too, chat about the
sexual organs of angels once in a while, you know?, I too
spend hours and hours talking about the Kafkaesque so and
so and the underground such and such, you know?, I'm not
criticising it, that, never, of course not, it would be like
criticising myself, ha! ha! ha!, but, of course, it is after all
clear that, well, that I think he is here for something, let's
say, more specific, isn't he?, I mean he is here thanks to my
hard work, well, it was mine, the idea that is, and we agreed
that nothing would happen if you . . . that since he was
more your friend than mine, much more yours than mine,
well, let's be clear about this, that since he was ONLY your
friend, and perhaps that's the point, I mean the funny thing,
well that, that you would suggest it to him in the quickest
and most direct way possible, right?, that yes, I mean
between neoclassical geometry, philoaesthetic
contemplation and and and and Parsifal's disease, you
might well have found a little space to explain everything
we've planned for him tonight, you know? . . . That's all.

Darkness.

Scene Eighteen

Lights. **The Female Friend**, *by herself, still, in the centre of the
room with a handbag. She seems nervous, or shy. She looks at the floor.
She crouches down. She stretches her hand out along the floor,
mechanically. She gets up. She coughs, as though she wanted to attract
somebody's attention. She smiles. She coughs again. She smiles. She
coughs again. The grimace on her face turns into a pout. She holds back
her tears. She walks towards the bed saying:*

The Female Friend   Hello . . . ?

Suddenly, a deafening scream is heard. **The Female Friend** *gets scared and jumps back, staring at the bed with a look of terror, as if it were the bed itself which had screamed.*

Darkness.

Scene Nineteen

Lights. **The Woman**, *kneeling down, is cleaning a part of the bedroom floor with a damp cloth.*

The Woman   Clean. Clean. Clean. Clean.
Clean floor.
Clean room.
I am clean.
Everything is clean.
It has to be clean.
Yes. Yes. Yes. Yes.

Pause. She gets up. She looks at the cloth with a certain 'distance'.

Ugh!
What a stink.
How revolting.
And how dissssgusting.
And that lad, with all his good looks.

Darkness.

Scene Twenty

Lights. **The Woman**, *kneeling down, is cleaning a part (the same one) of the bedroom floor with a damp cloth.*

The Woman   Clean. Clean. Clean. Clean.
Clean floor.
Clean room.
I am clean.
Everything is clean.

It has to be clean.
Yes. Yes. Yes. Yes.

Pause. She gets up. She looks at the cloth with a certain disgust.

Ugh!
What a stink.
How revolting.
And how dissssgusting.
And that lad, with all his good looks.

Pause.

Oh! . . . I just don't understand it . . . !

Scene Twenty-One

The Female Friend, *by herself, upstage. She looks to the right and to the left, as if she were looking for somebody. She carries a handbag.*

The Female Friend   May I?

She takes a few steps forward, timidly.

It's just that the door . . . I took it upon myself . . . and . . . since . . . hello? . . . since it was . . . hello? . . . I came so quickly that . . . and since it was open . . . well . . . Yes? . . . Is anyone there?

She stops. Pause. She looks at the floor. She crouches down. She gets up again. Facing the audience.

Oh, isn't this something, what a bundle of nerves I am . . .

Pause. She turns timidly and sees the bed. She looks ahead. She looks at the bed again, etc. (she wonders: 'oh, and what can that be?'). She bends over to take a better look at it (she appears to be extremely short-sighted). She thinks something ('could it be a table?'). Finally, with abnormal speed, she opens her handbag and takes out a pair of glasses. She puts them on and looks at the bed with a sudden gesture.

Oh. A bed? Yes, of course . . .

She takes off her glasses quickly and conceals them in the bag. She looks around as though she were afraid somebody may have seen her. Pause. She walks around the bedroom absent-mindedly. She sees a part of the floor that is wet. To check, she crouches down and touches the floor with her hand. She gets up. She coughs to attract somebody's attention. She smiles. She coughs again. She smiles, but less. She coughs again. She feels lonely and is unable to hold back her tears. She walks towards the bed and says:

Hello . . . ?

Suddenly, **The Woman** *screams from inside.* **The Female Friend** *looks at the bed and gets scared.*

Voice of The Woman   Ahhh!! Dear, are you already here?

The Female Friend   . . . Oh, yes . . , it's just that . . . I came . . . straight away and . . . oh.

Voice of The Woman   Oh, I'm coming, I'm coming, I'll be out in just a minute, right now, right now, just a moment, I'm in the middle of doing the washing!

The Female Friend   Don't . . . don't . . . don't worry about me . . . Go, go right ahead . . . don't . . . don't worry about me . . . I'll wait here, I'm just fine . . . oh yes.

Scene Twenty-Two

The Woman, **The Man** *and* **The Male Friend**. *All three, forming a semicircle, facing the audience.* **The Woman** *speaks to* **The Man**.

The Woman   . . . It just so happens that he's here, among other things, for this thing, which of course is my idea, therefore, if he is here it is thanks to me, and, of course, I don't mind if you waste saliva on your concept of a 'sub-realist' aesthetic, of course not!, on the other hand there are some things which really get me going, you know?, that really turn me on, you know?, what I mean is, I do it too,

chat about the sexual organs of angels once in a while, you
know?, I too spend hours and hours talking about the
Kafkaesque so and so and the underground such and such,
you know?, I'm not criticising it, that, never, of course not, it
would be like criticising myself, ha! ha! ha!, but, of course, it
is after all clear that, well, that I think he is here for
something, let's say, more specific, isn't he?, I mean he is
here thanks to my hard work, well, it was mine, the idea
that is, and we agreed that nothing would happen if you . . .,
that since he was more your friend than mine, much more
yours than mine, well, let's be clear about this, that since he
was only your friend, and perhaps that's the point, I mean
the funny thing, well that, that you would suggest it to him
in the quickest and most direct way possible, right?, that
yes, I mean between neoclassical geometry, philoaesthetic
contemplation and and and and Parsifal's disease, you
might well have found a little space to explain everything
we've planned for him tonight, you know? . . . That's
all.

The Man   Yes, you are absolutely right.

Pause.

The Woman   And now . . . ?

Pause.

The Woman   . . . WHO'S THE ONE WHO'S GOING
TO CLEAN UP ALL THIS SHIT?

Pause. **The Man** *and* **The Male Friend** *are left staring at*
The Woman.

The Woman   What a nerve!

Scene Twenty-Three

The Woman *and* **The Female Friend**. *They give each other a kiss on the cheek.*

The Woman   Darling! So sorry to keep you waiting!

The Female Friend   That's quite all right.

The Woman   Now, I'll explain everything, don't worry.

The Female Friend   I'm not worried about anything.

The Woman   What did you say? Are you feeling all right, dear?

The Female Friend   A little nervous, but I'm fine, thanks, it's nothing, nothing, it's just that I'm a bit anxious.

The Woman *takes* **The Female Friend** *by the arm and enthusiastically accompanies her over to the bed.*

The Woman   Et voilà!

The Female Friend   Ah.

Pause.

The Woman   Well, what do you think?

The Female Friend   It's so . . . so . . . so big, isn't it?

Pause.

The Woman   Yes.

Pause. **The Woman** *goes towards the bed.* **The Female Friend** *also moves closer to the bed. Both of them stand still on either side of the bed.*

The Woman   Do you like the sheets?

The Female Friend   Where did you buy them?

Pause.

The Woman   Do you like the sheets?

The Female Friend   You must have had them made to measure, mustn't you?

The Woman   Do you like the sheets?

The Female Friend   Aren't there any blankets?

Pause.

The Woman   Do you like the sheets?

The Female Friend   And wasn't it difficult to make up the bed on your own?

The Woman   Do you like the sheets?

The Female Friend   And won't you have pillows?

The Woman   Do you like the sheets?

The Female Friend   Isn't that an interesting colour scheme?

The Woman   Do you like the sheets?

The Female Friend   What kind of fabric are they? Cotton or a polyester blend?

The Woman   Do you like the sheets?!!

The Female Friend   No.

Pause. **The Woman** *stares severely at* **The Female Friend**. *Pause.* **The Woman** *goes up to* **The Female Friend**.

The Woman   You've been looking rather thin lately. You can't have been eating properly, I can tell from the colour of your face. Have you looked at yourself in the mirror lately? Your skin is drier than ever and your cheekbones look awfully prominent, jutting out. Deep wrinkles are visible at the corners of your eyes, and you've already got dark rings under them like bin-bags. Have you been to the doctor? You've got to, got to, got to go, please, in case you're suffering from something serious. Extremely serious. Oh, look at you!, look at you, you've got some kind of yellow scaly thing underneath your lips, on your chin, and you

have all that chafing on your neck! Malnutrition?
Exhaustion? Stress? Anxiety? . . . No, I know what it is:
neglect! Oh, I don't believe it. Ugh!, and that hair?! You
look absolutely terrible. We'll have to do something about
this, because if we don't . . .

The Female Friend You know what?, I hadn't even
noticed, I hadn't even noticed, but now that I can see them
better, now that I've had a more careful look at them . . . I
love your sheets!

The Woman Oh, really? I knew it, I knew you would like
them.

The Female Friend I mean I *really* like them. They're so
nice and I hadn't even realised.

Pause.

The Female Friend And so, now what?

The Woman It's better if he tells you about it.

Scene Twenty-Four

The Man *and* **The Male Friend**. **The Male Friend** *is
crying*.

The Man You're crying.

The Male Friend Tears of joy. I'm so moved.

The Man You make me so happy.

The Male Friend You're a genius, you're a genius,
you're a genius, kiss me, my friend, my head is spinning,
come, come and give me a hug, my friend, I need you to
touch me, grab me, take me in your arms because I think
I'm going dizzy! It must be . . . it must be . . . because of the
impact, I think I've got . . . I'm getting . . . THE
STENDHAL SYNDROME!

The Man What's that?

The Male Friend   Over-excitement in aesthetic contemplation, a physico-somatic disturbance when in the presence of Sublime Beauty! Oh, I can't take it any more, touch me, grab me, take me in your arms, genius-friend, ah! . . . Aaah!

The Male Friend *vomits noisily on the floor.* **The Man** *is left staring impassively at the vomit, which is already spreading on the floor.*

Scene Twenty-Five

The Man, **The Woman**, *and* **The Female Friend**.

The Man   And there you have it in a nutshell.

The Female Friend   Oh.

The Woman   What do you think?

Pause.

The Female Friend   Yes, yes, yes, a brilliant idea . . .

The Woman   I knew it. It was mine.

The Female Friend   . . . A superb idea, exciting, different, brilliant, yes, and I know, I know, I can see it now, yes, tomorrow, tomorrow, everything will have changed and life will be different and I'll be different, and it's about time too, oh, yes, and you know what?, I could already sense it, my intuition told me, earlier, just a couple of hours ago, and I was at home, in my flat, yes, you know, with nothing to do after work, lazing around, and then, suddenly, flash!, without knowing how or why I saw everything: something came over me and I knew it, something was about to happen, it would finally happen to me, and do you know why?, do you know why I know now or I knew then, yes, a couple of hours ago, at home all by myself in my nice little flat?, look, it's very simple, it's very simple, it was nothing, so, without rhyme or reason, no explanation or anything, my heart started pounding, an immense pounding, like this,

like this: BABAM! BABAM!, and you see, I got scared, at
first: oh no, a heart attack!, I thought, but it wasn't, but it
wasn't, but it wasn't, because right afterwards, RING,
RING, RING, the sound of the phone, and I go running
like mad to grab it DADADA, DADADA DADADA, and
'yes?, hello, who is it?', and then your voice so convincing,
so so so firmly categorical: 'come over straight away, I need
to show you something and make you an offer . . .', and,
there you have it, at that moment I said to myself, a sign, a
sign, my sudden beating heart was a sign, I saw it all, all of a
sudden, like a revelation, tonight, I saw it clearly, sharply
and all all just when I hung up the phone, and without
anyone telling me about it, tonight . . . tonight . . . that's
why I was so flustered when I came here . . . tonight . . .

The Woman   A real début.

The Female Friend   Oh, I'd been waiting for so long for
something like this, an experience like this, a night like this,
a complete turnaround, a radical change in my boring,
godforsaken life! Oh, and it's all thanks to you, darling.
Here, give me a hug, give me a hug.

The Female Friend *walks towards* **The Woman** *with open*
arms and a smile of gratitude, but when she steps on the wet spot, she
spectacularly slips and falls flat on her back. **The Woman** *screams*
and goes to help her, but as she comes near, she too slips and her legs fly
open. **The Female Friend** *gets up and shrieks when she sees*
The Woman *on the floor.* **The Woman** *asks for help, stretching*
out her arms. **The Female Friend** *tries to lift her up but she*
cannot. There is a tottering struggle between them, amid cries of
desperation from both women. Finally, **The Woman** *swiftly yanks*
the arm of **The Female Friend** *in one final attempt to lift herself*
up. **The Female Friend** *ends up falling on top of her. Hysterical*
screams from both of them. All the while, **The Man***, who for some*
time has been paying no attention to what **The Female Friend**
has been saying, seems to have discovered an irregularity in one of the
legs of the bed. He has bent over and is meticulously examining the leg.
He does not seem to have noticed anything else that has been going on,
busy and preoccupied as he is with the bed.

The Man   I think something's cracked.

The Woman *finally gets up with an almost superhuman effort.*

The Woman   It's the windows' fault, the windows, there aren't any windows, there aren't any, and there isn't any ventilation, and this hasn't dried up yet, shit! That . . . shitty Parsifal!

The Female Friend   Yes, I think I'm the one who's cracked.

The Man   The leg.

The Woman   Good God!

Scene Twenty-Six

The Man *and* **The Woman**. *A shoe on the floor, and near it,* **The Woman** *stretched out with a leg in the air.* **The Man** *is giving her a foot massage, with absolute tenderness.*

The Woman   Did you understand, or didn't you?

The Man   Yes. Well, not really.

The Woman   Sometimes I really think you're an idiot. Didn't we want a really big début, a solemn inauguration, tonight, this very night?

Pause.

The Man   OK?

The Woman   Yes.

Pause.

The Woman   He is nice-looking and she is nice-looking, he is young and she is young.

The Man   Is that OK?

The Woman   Yes.

Pause.

The Woman   It couldn't be more perfect, more complete:
a real first-night début, the thing's début and their début,
the début of a couple for a début, in the début they'll be
making a début themselves, by making a début themselves
they'll be giving it a début, by giving it a début, they'll be
making a début themselves, it is THE DÉBUT BY
MAKING A DÉBUT.

Pause.

The Woman   Oh, sometimes I'm just so incredible.

The Man *violently grabs* **The Woman**'s *foot and gives it a sharp
tug.*

The Woman   Ouch! That hurts! Oh, you've hurt me!
You beast!

The Man   Just a little jolt to put everything in place.

The Woman   Do you expect me to believe that?

The Man   Of course.

The Woman   What's the matter?, you're upset it was
mine and not yours, aren't you? The idea, that is. That's it,
isn't it?

She gets up and puts on her shoe. She slaps him violently.

The Woman   This is your sweet revenge, eh? You did it
on purpose, didn't you?

The Man   No.

The Woman   Well, it seemed that way to me, all the signs
were there.

The Man   You're right, I did it on purpose, but it was for
your own good, to fix it for you, that's the way it's done,
believe me, one swift blow. Try it and you'll see.

The Woman *takes a few steps. Carefully.*

The Man Better?

The Woman Better.

The Man You see?

The Woman Thank you and I'm sorry.

Pause.

The Woman Well, let's get on with it: you take care of him and I'll take care of her.

Scene Twenty-Seven

The Male Friend, *by himself, at the back of the bedroom with a key in his hand. He walks towards the audience.*

The Male Friend Hey? Oh? Good evening good evening? . . . It's not a good evening? . . . Oh, never mind. Oh . . . never mind. Too early. Why am I always so reliable and oh, so polite, so perfect?

He looks at his watch.

So perfect that I'm early, yes, I'm early in everything, as always, I'm really what they call an earlycomer. Twenty. Minutes.

Pause. He looks at the key. He puts it in his trouser pocket. He forces his hand deep into his pocket as if it were hard to get the key into it. He takes out his hand. He moves his fingers (they are sticky). He smells them. He looks at them. He smells them again. He looks at his pocket.

Oh. What a stench. Mouldy.

Pause. He looks at the bed.

Fantastic.

Pause. He looks at his body, his hands.

Not sweets. Or flowers. Or champagne either. I'm a man of my time.

He looks at the bed.

Like you. Nothing ornamental or frivolous, nothing but our very own integrity intact, without any revolting romanticism, or absurd little gifts. Yes, you are perfect, too. Because you're like me, I'm like you and I've come too early, since the two of us are ahead of the game, on the cutting edge of our time, I haven't brought anything, like you, and I'm going out for a walk, oh, don't you worry, I'll be back, my bed-friend, for you, for you and with nothing, stripped naked in front of you and in front of . . . her, without frivolity or extravagance, without gifts, and God I'm hot and I'm leaving, the impact is too intense when I look at you and the unknown woman is unknown and that's why she'll be late, I bet she's a latecomer, of course, she's a woman, what do you expect, they knew how to sell her to me, my brother, but they don't know the truth, that I'm not here for the latecomer, but for you, and I've agreed to it for you, and I'll do everything for you, only for you, my soul-brother, my equal.

Pause.

Keep my secret.

Pause.

The secret between a man and . . . an object, like the secret between a man and another man.

Pause.

I love you.

Scene Twenty-Eight

The Woman, *by herself, moving around the bed in circles.*

The Woman   How can I make fun of Ill-Fated Destiny? Destiny! Oh fucking destiny! Fucking bed! And fucking sheets! Fucking evening and all that time wasted! Oh, yes, fucking everything!

With an attack of furious rage, she begins to kick the bed. For a good while. Suddenly, she remains still – she has doubtless hurt herself – and without the slightest sound of pain, with complete dignity, she arranges her dress, her hair, etc. She hobbles around the bed.

Oh, I've hurt myself.

She continues limping around the bed.

It had to be like this.

Pause.

And now, on top of everything, crippled for the rest of my life. It had to be like this, of course. It was also in the stars that I'd have to have my leg amputated, that was also in the stars. Just like everything else. Everything was in the stars. Yes, everything in the . . . stars!

She stops.

But . . . and if . . . ? Yes! Yes! Oh, now I've got it, I've got it!

Her face radiates with joy. She calms down. And, suddenly, she remembers her foot hurts.

Ah! Ah! Ah! Oh! Help! It hurts! Oh! I've hurt myself! Help!! My foot, my foot, my foot!! . . .

Scene Twenty-Nine

The Female Friend, *at the back of the bedroom. She walks towards the audience. She is nervous.*

Female Friend   Hello . . . ?

Pause. She looks all around. She relaxes. Suddenly, she energetically scratches her armpits and her breasts.

Oh, this damn thing won't stop itching! I feel so so so hemmed in and constrained . . . ! Oh!

Suddenly, she stops and remains still.

Oh, could he be hiding somewhere and spying on me?!

She looks under the bed.

No. Ugh.

Pause.

Ha, ha. And now what? And now what? Wait for him. Oh.
Excitement? Intrigue? And what, what will he be like?, I'm
dying to know. Probably handsome, masculine, charming
and a bit of a sadist. Ah, yes, yes, yes, if everything goes
well, (it will, I'm sure), tomorrow I'll give up, yes, I'll give up
my job, I'll tell them categorically: 'go to hell all of you, my
life has changed, and I'm not dreaming, it's wonderful,
exciting, different, and I'm leaving and you can all stay
here, you're a bunch of boring louts!' Oh. Ha!, ha!, ha!
Sometimes I'm so ADVENTUROUS and so so so wild!
Oh, what fun! I can't wait to see their faces . . . they're going
to be left right in the lurch . . . and how they'll hate me . . . !!

Pause.

Hey, he's awfully late, isn't he? Ahhh, it's better that way, it
increases the expectation, the excitement, the . . . LIBIDO,
well. Ah . . . the chance of a lifetime!

Pause.

Let's see, let's go over everything one last time: first of all,
don't look dull; secondly, be natural, spontaneous,
spectacular, divine and feminine at all times; thirdly, don't
put my glasses on (that's most important because if he sees
me with my glasses, he'll never get it up); fourthly, I've got
to appear totally lewd, corrupt and degenerate. Oh, I'll be a
provocative bitch, he'll love it, he'll love it. Yes . . . it could
be exciting, yes, more exciting if I do the bitch thing, yes,
much more, much more. Yes, yes, yes, my great
opportunity.

She adopts a lewd and provocative pose. She sticks out her tongue.

Yoo hoo!

She walks about awkwardly, trying to be what she is not and cannot be, with her eyes on the door.

Good evening . . .

She stops. She comes out of the pose.

Oh, no, no, even better!

She takes off her clothes as if she were trying to perform a very sexy strip-tease. But it turns out to be absolutely ridiculous and even pathetic. She stands in her bra and knickers.

Hello, how're you doing?

The rattling of some keys in the lock of the door. Noise of the door opening and shutting. **The Female Friend**, *who was practically in a state of ecstasy, realises that it is* **The Male Friend** *who is coming in. She reacts suddenly and, since she does not have time to get dressed, a look of terror appears on her face and she lets out a muffled scream.*

Scene Thirty

The Man *and* **The Woman**.

The Woman   I've got a theory.

The Man   About what?

The Woman   About what's happening.

The Man   Tell me.

The Woman   Do you know who's to blame?

The Man   For what?

The Woman   For what's just happened to us.

The Man   No. Who?

The Woman   I don't know if I should tell you.

The Man   Why?

The Woman   Because I know you'll laugh.

The Man   I won't laugh.

The Woman   You will laugh.

The Man   Whose fault is it? Mine?

The Woman   No. Not yours.

The Man   Whose is it, then?

The Woman   It's DESTINY's fault!, fucking destiny, it doesn't like me, it doesn't like you, it doesn't like us,

She points to the bed.

it doesn't like it and, as a result, it's a bad sign!, I'm telling you, believe me, it's a bad sign when destiny doesn't like you, that destiny goes and fucks with you, like it's just fucked with us now: it fucks with me by telephone and it fucks with you by telephone, too; destiny almost always fucks with you by telephone, you can see how amusing the whole thing is, can't you?; because the person who just called me was not my brother-in-law telling me tonight my sister's going to have an operation and I have to spend the night with her at the hospital, oh, no, no, just like the person who just called you was not your boss telling you that it's today and not three weeks from now that you have to begin the night shift, oh, no, no, it wasn't my brother-in-law or your boss, no!, it was the voice of destiny, of TRAGIC DESTINY, which diabolically disguised itself as my brother-in-law and your boss, and went over our heads to bog us down and fuck us up and play such a dirty trick on us, so we wouldn't be able to give it its début tonight. Fucking destiny.

Pause.

The Man   It's not so tragic.

The Woman   If it's not so tragic for you that destiny is working against us and doing us harm, then we might as well just call the whole thing off once and for all.

Pause.

The Woman   Alone! Leave me alone!

Scene Thirty-One

The Male Friend, *holding a key, and* **The Female Friend**. *He has just surprised her in her underwear.*

The Male Friend   Hello.

The Female Friend   Hello.

Pause. **The Female Friend** *tries to cover up the awkwardness of the situation. In spite of this,* **The Male Friend** *also feels uncomfortable and surprised.*

The Male Friend   Pleased to meet you. I'm sorry I'm late. But, in fact, I came earlier. Much earlier. So, I'm not running late and I'm not a latecomer either. I just went out for a walk. You see, I had already come. You hadn't yet. That's precisely why I went for a walk. Pleased to meet you. To get some fresh air.

The Female Friend   I had a hot flush, as well.

The Male Friend   Right. And a key, as well.

The Female Friend   I was finding the heat rather oppressive, as you can see.

The Male Friend   Yes, yes, I can see. And you had a key, as well.

The Female Friend   As well. Ha, ha, delighted to meet you.

The Male Friend   Right.

They shake hands, clumsily. The key falls from **The Male Friend***'s hand. He picks it up and puts it in his trouser pocket.* **The Female Friend** *misinterprets his gesture and gives him a stare that is intended to be provocative.* **The Male Friend** *coughs, perhaps uncomfortably, rather coldly.* **The Female Friend** *misinterprets his attitude.*

The Female Friend   Well, then . . .

The Female Friend *places her hands behind her to undo her bra.* **The Male Friend** *does not understand anything that is going on. Suddenly,* **The Female Friend** *becomes engaged in a serious struggle to undo her bra.* **The Male Friend** *does not laugh, nor does he make the slightest gesture to help her or to go near her.* **The Female Friend***, indirectly, asks him for help and continues to struggle with her bra. The fight is already a feverish war with the bra and she is already sweating, she despairs in silence, gasps and nearly chokes.* **The Male Friend** *tries to help her, but immediately he has had enough. Unmoved, he sits down on the floor and calmly, takes out a cigarette, lights it and smokes. He contemplates, entranced, the smoke that he elegantly exhales.* **The Female Friend***, weakened from the battle with her bra, takes her aching hands from behind her back, looks at them and lets out a cry of desperation.*

The Female Friend   Aaaah! Help me, help me, help me, help me. I can't, can't you see?, I can't do it, there's a resistance, a contrary force, reactionary, contrary to the impulse, to the natural impulse, to the impulse I have, that comes from inside me, and it's preventing me, you see, oh, what shit!, you saw, how embarrassing, you saw, didn't you?, or no, or perhaps not?, but, so, the thing is there's no way, it won't open, it doesn't want to, yes, yes, that's it, it's the one who doesn't want to, oh, not me!, it's not me, you saw, didn't you?, oh, it doesn't want to, it won't let me, it's keeping me from, what?, oh!, bloody reactionary thing!, and it's also the fault of the fucking, this fucking thing in the back, yes, that's it, it's the one, and it's also this other thing, it's their fault, the BRA and the CLIP, the fucking clip, this clip that you can't see, you haven't seen, but it's there, here in the back, revolting, difficult, screwed-up, twisted, it hates me, it hates me and that's why it's burning my fingers, the bloody clip, it's destroying them, this fucking clip, you see, it goes on like a mad woman, like a strait-laced nun that won't open, it doesn't want to open, it doesn't want to, it's a hook with two hooks that grip each other, then come together, intertwine and they won't let anyone anyone anyone take them apart, not a finger, no, not a finger of mine, not one of mine, not one of my fingers can unfasten it, and look at what's happened to them: reddish, black and blue, hurting, frustrated!, oh you absurd hook!, and do you know what?, do you know the best part?, that, this afternoon, yes, this very afternoon, when I left this place, I bought it for you, this REACTIONARY bra, yes, for you and for you, and now it doesn't want to, it won't let me, it doesn't want to, it's rebelling against me. It doesn't want to . . . let me show them to you.

The Male Friend   Show them to me?

The Female Friend   My breasts.

The Male Friend   Oh.

Pause. He puts out his cigarette on the floor, slowly.

Listen . . . and who told you that I wanted to . . . ?, that I wanted you to . . . that your . . . that you would . . . ?

Pause.

The Female Friend   I'm cold.

The Male Friend   Right.

The Female Friend   And I'm going to the lavatory.

The Male Friend   Oh, OK. Female matters, women's business.

The Female Friend   What?

The Male Friend   Your period?

The Female Friend   No.

Pause.

For a shit.

Scene Thirty-Two

The Woman, *contemplating the bed from a distance, nervous, in a bad mood, overexcited.*

The Woman   Oh!, what a mess and what a disaster, oh, how awful, how awful!

Suddenly, something comes over her, a kind of hysterical fit, and she flings herself towards the bed as though she were insane. She tears off the sheets and brutally throws them on the floor. Pause. She has a wild expression on her face. She exhales. She seems to calm down. She looks at the bed and the sheets. She closes her eyes as if she were forcing herself to calm down, to concentrate.

A second time, a second time.

Pause.

Everything always turns out great the second time round.

Pause.

Now, come on!

Scene Thirty-Three

The Male Friend, *by himself.*

The Male Friend   I can go to the chemist's!

Pause.

Well, I don't think she can hear me. What do you know, the unknown woman has turned out to be hysterical, histrionic and absurdly romantic, a strange specimen, a scatter-brained romantic, ridiculously old-fashioned, and I think

I'm getting bored, and that I'm falling asleep and I don't know what the hell I'm doing here.

He looks at the bed.

Excuse me. It was a small oversight, don't think I forgot about you.

Pause.

But, what should I do?: to kill or not to kill time?, to go or not to go, that is the question and tomorrow I've got a lot of work to do, oh, I am so tired, but no, no, I don't want to infect you with my lethargy, my friend.

Pause. To the bed.

I know what you're thinking: what a night and how odd, right?, two lost souls, especially her, two strangers, and you right in the middle, imposing, thinking: 'what are they doing here, two strangers in the night?' Oh, two strangers in the night . . . let's kill some time . . .

He starts singing, with a terrible accent and a sense of pitch that is even worse, a song that 'is intended to sound' like 'Strangers in the Night'. Just when he has finished singing, he sits down, and the loud flushing of a lavatory can be heard.

Scene Thirty-Four

Lights. **The Man** *and* **The Woman**.

The Woman   Oh! It's not heavy! It's not heavy, it's not heavy!! How marvellous! It's not heavy.

The Man   If you remember . . . we agreed that it was important for it to be simple. Light. Agile. Light. Dynamic. And light. Forgoing all complications. And extravagances. Light. Yes. Light. But solid, too. In its own way.

Pause.

And here it is.

Pause.

Just like that.

Scene Thirty-Five

The Male Friend *and* **The Female Friend**. **The Female Friend**, *having just emerged from the lavatory, in her knickers and one of* **The Woman**'s *night shirts.*

The Female Friend   I didn't know you were a singer.

The Male Friend   I'm not.

The Female Friend   You sing quite well.

The Male Friend   Well, there you are.

The Female Friend   There you are.

Pause.

The Male Friend   I enjoy singing. That's all. There's no mystery to it: when I sing I enjoy myself, when I'm enjoying myself, I sing, I sing to enjoy myself and I sing when I'm bored.

The Female Friend   Oh.

Pause.

The Male Friend   A cigarette?

The Female Friend   Shall we talk?

The Male Friend   A cigarette?

The Female Friend   Shall we sit down?

The Male Friend   What?!

Pause. **The Male Friend** *glares severely at her. He lights up a cigarette and smokes.*

The Female Friend   A cigarette.

The Male Friend *gives her a cigarette and moves away from her.*

The Female Friend   A light.

The Male Friend   What?

The Female Friend   Hmm . . . A light.

The Male Friend   Excuse me?

The Female Friend   I would like to smoke it.

The Male Friend   Oh.

The Male Friend *gives her a lighter.* **The Female Friend**
*lights the cigarette and gives the lighter back to him. She is very
suggestive: she closes her eyes and offers him her mouth.* **The Male
Friend**, *with an obvious effort, brings his mouth close to hers, to kiss
her, but he stops when he sees the ridiculous expression on her face. He
moves away from her with large strides. She tries to hide her
embarrassment.*

The Female Friend   Hey, ha ha.

Pause.

Have you noticed? There's not a single chair in this
bedroom.

The Male Friend   In this BEAUTIFUL bedroom.

The Female Friend   Yes.

The Male Friend   No. There aren't any.

The Female Friend   No.

The Male Friend   That's the way it is. Austerity, austere,
austerityaboveallelse . . .

The Female Friend   Of course, of course.

The Male Friend   Just a bed. Because this is a bedroom.
Not a living-room. Not a dining-room. Just as it should be.

The Female Friend   Right.

Pause.

The Female Friend   Because . . . of course, it would be absurd, wouldn't it?, for you and me . . . you and me . . . to sit on it now, wouldn't it?

The Male Friend   I hope you're not serious, I hope and wish that it's merely a whim, a passing thought, for a brief, fleeting, spontaneous moment. A joke, ehemm . . . in bad taste. THIS IS A BED. Not a chair. Not a divan. Not a stool. Not a sofa. Not a pouffe.

The Female Friend   Just what I was saying: it would be absurd.

The Male Friend   It would be unforgivable. Imagine the situation just for a moment, please: you and me, perfect strangers, without knowing what to say to each other, without daring to look at each other, talking about the weather or about the whims of chance, you on the left and me on the right, arms folded in front of us so they don't betray the awkwardness of this stupid conversation and, above all, the most incredible thing about it, the most intolerable thing: WITH OUR LEGS HANGING OVER THE EDGE! Imagine!

The Female Friend   Oh, yes, how horrible!

The Male Friend   It would be . . .

The Female Friend   It would be unforgivable.

The Male Friend   . . . An absolute betrayal.

Pause.

The Female Friend   Excuse me . . . you said . . . a betrayal? A . . . betrayal? Hmm . . . of who? Hmm . . . of what? Hmm . . . it, no, never mind, I'm not interested, you know?, well, actually, I am very interested, you know?, in knowing why . . . you think, you could possibly think or consider that you and me sitting here with our . . . (how embarrassing, really, now I can see, ah, yes, now I can see, oh) . . . with our . . . legs . . . like that . . ., dangling (it really is something, isn't it, it really is wild, don't you think?) . . .

would be . . . a . . . betrayal . . . No, and I mean I'm
interested, you know?, because, of course, I personally find
the whole thing absolutely preposterous, out of proportion
as an image, don't you think?, I mean I find it ridiculous
and much more, you know?, but of course, come on . . .
betrayal betrayal perhaps . . . perhaps not so much, you
know?, of course God knows, you know?, God knows what
you were thinking when you said that, you know?, but go
on, it's just that in fact I don't know if I really understand
you completely: which for me is rather embarrassing, it just
so happens that for you it is a betrayal . . . no, no I've
already told you: I'm interested, you know?, don't take it the
wrong way, I'm interested perhaps in knowing what the hell
could have compelled you to say so, and let it be said in
passing, to say so in that way – how should I say? – which
was so well put, wasn't it?, so strongly, well, yes, yes, I mean
that if you don't mind, well . . . that there must be an
explanation, I think . . . or perhaps not . . . what what what
what were you referring to when you mentioned a . . .
'betrayal'?

Pause.

The Male Friend   You and me sitting here, on it. A
betrayal of the bed, obviously.

The Female Friend   Oh, yes, the bed, of course. What
else could it have been? Excuse me: WHO else could it have
been?

The Female Friend, *offended, gives him a severe look.* **The
Male Friend** *puts out his cigarette on the floor. She observes him
now with an air of superiority.*

The Female Friend   Hmm . . . a slight problem, just a
slight problem: if you are you and I am me, and the bed is a
bed (above all the bed, of course, which is a bed and nothing
more, as I already know very well thanks to you), so, here, in
my opinion, this place where we are right now should be a
BEDROOM AND NOT AN ASHTRAY.

Quickly, **The Male Friend**, *embarrassed, picks up the cigarette butts from the floor and blows on the ashes.* **The Female Friend** *looks at him and, ceremoniously, puts out her cigarette on the sole of her shoe and offers it to him with a certain aloofness.*

The Female Friend   A present.

The Male Friend   Thank you.

The Female Friend   Don't mention it.

The Female Friend *places the extinguished cigarette in* **The Male Friend***'s outstretched hand, next to the others. Both of them remain silent, staring at the cigarette butts.*

The Male Friend/The Female Friend   What a stench!

The Male Friend   Sorry?

The Female Friend   What?

The Male Friend   No, nothing.

The Female Friend   Me neither, then.

The Male Friend   Very well, then.

The Female Friend   Well yes.

Pause. **The Male Friend** *yawns unashamedly. When* **The Female Friend** *sees this, she suddenly feels insulted: degraded. She moves away from him with tears in her eyes. Pause. The two of them end up stretching out on the floor.* **The Female Friend** *once again catches the attention of* **The Male Friend** *in order to return the yawn.*

Scene Thirty-Six

The Man, *behind the bed, facing the audience.*

The Man   Two by two . . .

Pause. Very quickly:

Sorry? What? Excuse me? Oh, yes, yes: the advantages of a
two-by-two metre bed?: all of them, to say it in a
deliberately simplistic way. Blah blah blah. Blah blah blah.
Blah blah blah.

Pause.

Blah.

Pause.

Blah blah of the opposite sex . . .

Pause.

Yes. Of the opposite sex.

Pause.

Opposite . . . sex. The opposite . . . sex, the sex of the
opposite, of the opposite sex. Yes.

Pause.

The first . . . conclusion . . . well: bah!

Scene Thirty-Seven

The Male Friend, **The Female Friend**, **The Man** *and*
The Woman. **The Man** *and* **The Woman** *have just entered
the room. It is daytime.* **The Male Friend** *and* **The Female
Friend** *are stretched out on the floor, in a deep slumber.* **The Man**
and **The Woman** *stand and observe them in astonishment.*

The Woman   But what's all this?!!

The Man   Your idea on the floor.

The Woman   Shut up, you bloody fool, no one asked you
to speak!

The Man   And how is your dear sister?

The Woman   What difference does it make to you? Shit.

She turns and looks at the empty bed.

Oh, oh, untouched! Untouched! Untouched! But what's going on?, what's going on, or what's NOT going on? Oh, I think I'm going to have an attack!

The Man   I'm going to wake them up.

The Woman   Oh, nothing!, nothing!, nothing!, I'm going to go crazy! A bad sign, this is a bad sign, I know, I can feel it! There we have today's youth, snoring, sleeping on the floor with their legs spread out. Oh, how disgusting, there's no integrity here, or any self-esteem, or passion, or daring, or gallantry, nothing, oh!, impotent, diminished, null and void, yes, all of them wretched, godforsaken, impotent, nonentities!

The Man *first wakes up* **The Male Friend**, *and then* **The Female Friend**.

The Man   Wake up.

The Male Friend   Huh? Huh?

The Woman   I can't, I can't, I can't believe it!

The Man   Up, up, up, up, time to get up.

The Female Friend   Oh. Ah. I was . . . Oh, hello. Where . . . ? How . . . ? Ah, I was dreaming that . . . that they were . . .

The Woman   Dreaming, of course, dreaming . . .

The Woman, *whimpering, sits down on one of the corners of the bed.* **The Female Friend** *gets dressed.* **The Woman** *gives* **The Man** *a severe look.*

The Woman   You know what? You can keep it and you know what you can do with it.

The Man   What?

The Woman   YOUR bed. As far as I am concerned, you can stuff the whole thing.

The Man   What do you mean?

The Woman   I've just taken an irrevocable decision.

The Man   Are you feeling all right?

The Female Friend   Good . . . good evening.

The Woman   Good MORNING, my dear, good
MORNING, love, and wipe the sleep from your eyes.

The Male Friend   Hello . . . It's just that . . . that . . . I . . .
ah, it must be late, I . . . was . . . wasn't . . . feeling very well,
you know. I don't think she . . . she . . . either.

The Female Friend   Huh?

The Male Friend *sits down on one of the other corners of the bed.
He yawns.* **The Female Friend** *sits down on one of the other
corners. She yawns.* **The Woman** *gives* **The Man** *a severe look.*

The Woman   You don't need to pretend you're deaf.

The Man   I heard you perfectly.

The Man *sits down on the unoccupied corner. Silence.*

The Male Friend   I've got to go.

The Female Friend   I've got to go.

The Male Friend   I have to go to work.

The Female Friend   Me too. To work.

The Male Friend   I'm so tired.

The Female Friend   My back aches. It aches right here,
in my spine . . . Oh, it feels as if I . . . as if I'd . . .

The Woman   As if you'd NOTHING, love. Nothing at
all. Everything is just as it was! . . .

The Female Friend   I'm going.

The Male Friend   Me too.

The Woman   Me too!!

The Man   What?

The Woman   I'm going!!

The Man   Where?

The Woman   I mean I'm leaving, I mean I'm not going anywhere in particular, no, no, I mean I'm going away, in . . . in general, I mean . . . not at all. Everything has turned out so terribly . . .

The Female Friend *gets up, walks in front of* **The Man** *and* **The Woman**, *and goes towards* **The Male Friend**. *She holds out her hand to him.*

The Female Friend   Well, it's been a pleasure, you know?, a pleasure to meet you, I really have had an evening . . . ooh, a very . . . I mean, a night . . . really, it's been years and years and years and years since I've had, I can assure you, believe me!!!

The Male Friend   Yes, yes, me too. I mean . . . me neither.

The Male Friend *coughs.* **The Female Friend** *points to his trouser pocket. He puts his hand in and takes out three cigarette butts.*

The Male Friend   Hmm . . . of course . . . too much smoke.

The Female Friend   Right.

The Male Friend *gets up.*

The Male Friend   Goodbye.

The Female Friend   Goodbye.

The Man *looks at* **The Woman**, *very seriously.*

The Man   Goodbye, then!!

The Woman   Yes, goodbye, you impotent fool, the play is over. Between you and me. Between all of us, as far as I can see. Nothing turns out properly if it doesn't start properly and nothing changes, my dear nonentity. And there's no way your shitty bed is going to change the shit between us.

Between anyone! Yes, Destiny, when it fucks you up, really fucks you up right until the bitter end.

The Female Friend *puts her glasses on in order to look at her watch.*

The Female Friend   Oh, it's so late.

They all look at her.

Scene Thirty-Eight

The Man *and* **The Woman**.*

The Woman   Well, what? Well, then. What do you think. Shall I go? Is it clear to you or . . . or . . . or . . . or not. Come on, what do you think?

The Man   Goodbye.

The Woman   Oh.

The Man   Yes. Yes. Yes. You'd better go. Better. Better. Better.

The Woman   Well, then. Now it's definite: I'm going.

The Man   I'm sure that . . .

The Woman   That what?

Pause.

The Woman   If you need anything . . .

The Man   Hmm . . . At the moment, I don't know.

The Woman   Well, then, goodbye.

The Man   Wait.

The Woman   What?

The Man   Will you be long?

*Translator's note: the original Catalan version specifies that the bed no longer be on stage during this scene. The Castilian Spanish version does not make any such indication.

The Woman   Well, look, I don't know. I've got to go quite a long way. I may be.

The Man   Oh, so I don't think that . . .

The Woman   That what?

The Man   Are you sure you don't want . . . You prefer . . . ?

The Woman   It's just that I can't stay here any longer. I'm tired of doing nothing and I'm going to go and do what I should have done some time ago. I'm feeling very restless and stressed out, you know, so you stay here by yourself and I'll go. It'll be all right, in fact, just the opposite, it'll be better, because I know that . . .

The Man   Do you want me to go . . .

The Woman   No, no, no, no. You can't leave. You have to stay put. Just imagine if . . . Besides besides, I can do it by myself. By myself I can.

The Man   You mean?

The Woman   Of course! Of course, I can, you'll see, I don't think I'll get too tired, no, I don't think I'll get too tired, don't worry about me.

The Man   Fine, do what you want.

The Woman   Right. Come on then, that's enough pointless chattering away. (As always.) So . . . goodbye.

Pause.

Goodbye.

Pause.

Goodbye.

Pause.

GOODBYE.

The Woman *leaves.* **The Man** *is left by himself. Silence.*

The End

Methuen Modern Plays
include work by

Jean Anouilh
John Arden
Margaretta D'Arcy
Peter Barnes
Sebastian Barry
Brendan Behan
Dermot Bolger
Edward Bond
Bertolt Brecht
Howard Brenton
Anthony Burgess
Simon Burke
Jim Cartwright
Caryl Churchill
Noël Coward
Lucinda Coxon
Sarah Daniels
Nick Darke
Nick Dear
Shelagh Delaney
David Edgar
David Eldridge
Dario Fo
Michael Frayn
John Godber
Paul Godfrey
David Greig
John Guare
Peter Handke
David Harrower
Jonathan Harvey
Iain Heggie
Declan Hughes
Terry Johnson
Sarah Kane
Charlotte Keatley
Barrie Keeffe
Howard Korder

Robert Lepage
Stephen Lowe
Doug Lucie
Martin McDonagh
John McGrath
Terrence McNally
David Mamet
Patrick Marber
Arthur Miller
Mtwa, Ngema & Simon
Tom Murphy
Phyllis Nagy
Peter Nichols
Joseph O'Connor
Joe Orton
Louise Page
Joe Penhall
Luigi Pirandello
Stephen Poliakoff
Franca Rame
Mark Ravenhill
Philip Ridley
Reginald Rose
David Rudkin
Willy Russell
Jean-Paul Sartre
Sam Shepard
Wole Soyinka
Shelagh Stephenson
C. P. Taylor
Theatre de Complicite
Theatre Workshop
Sue Townsend
Judy Upton
Timberlake Wertenbaker
Roy Williams
Victoria Wood

Methuen Contemporary Dramatists
include

Peter Barnes (three volumes)
Sebastian Barry
Edward Bond (six volumes)
Howard Brenton
  (two volumes)
Richard Cameron
Jim Cartwright
Caryl Churchill (two volumes)
Sarah Daniels (two volumes)
Nick Darke
David Edgar (three volumes)
Ben Elton
Dario Fo (two volumes)
Michael Frayn (two volumes)
Paul Godfrey
John Guare
Peter Handke
Jonathan Harvey
Declan Hughes
Terry Johnson (two volumes)
Bernard-Marie Koltès
David Lan
Bryony Lavery
Doug Lucie
David Mamet (three volumes)

Martin McDonagh
Duncan McLean
Anthony Minghella
  (two volumes)
Tom Murphy (four volumes)
Phyllis Nagy
Anthony Nielsen
Philip Osment
Louise Page
Joe Penhall
Stephen Poliakoff
  (three volumes)
Christina Reid
Philip Ridley
Willy Russell
Ntozake Shange
Sam Shepard (two volumes)
Wole Soyinka (two volumes)
David Storey (three volumes)
Sue Townsend
Michel Vinaver (two volumes)
Michael Wilcox
David Wood (two volumes)
Victoria Wood

Methuen World Classics
include

Jean Anouilh (two volumes)
John Arden (two volumes)
Arden & D'Arcy
Brendan Behan
Aphra Behn
Bertolt Brecht (six volumes)
Büchner
Bulgakov
Calderón
Čapek
Anton Chekhov
Noël Coward (seven volumes)
Eduardo De Filippo
Max Frisch
John Galsworthy
Gogol
Gorky
Harley Granville Barker
   (two volumes)
Henrik Ibsen (six volumes)
Lorca (three volumes)

Marivaux
Mustapha Matura
David Mercer (two volumes)
Arthur Miller (five volumes)
Molière
Musset
Peter Nichols (two volumes)
Clifford Odets
Joe Orton
A. W. Pinero
Luigi Pirandello
Terence Rattigan
   (two volumes)
W. Somerset Maugham
   (two volumes)
August Strindberg
   (three volumes)
J. M. Synge
Ramón del Valle-Inclán
Frank Wedekind
Oscar Wilde

Methuen Classical Greek Dramatists

Aeschylus Plays: One
(Persians, Seven Against Thebes, Suppliants,
Prometheus Bound)

Aeschylus Plays: Two
(Oresteia: Agamemnon, Libation-Bearers, Eumenides)

Aristophanes Plays: One
(Acharnians, Knights, Peace, Lysistrata)

Aristophanes Plays: Two
(Wasps, Clouds, Birds, Festival Time, Frogs)

Aristophanes & Menander: New Comedy
(Women in Power, Wealth, The Malcontent,
The Woman from Samos)

Euripides Plays: One
(Medea, The Phoenician Women, Bacchae)

Euripides Plays: Two
(Hecuba, The Women of Troy, Iphigeneia at Aulis,
Cyclops)

Euripides Plays: Three
(Alkestis, Helen, Ion)

Euripides Plays: Four
(Elektra, Orestes, Iphigeneia in Tauris)

Euripides Plays: Five
(Andromache, Herakles' Children, Herakles)

Euripides Plays: Six
(Hippolytos, Suppliants, Rhesos)

Sophocles Plays: One
(Oedipus the King, Oedipus at Colonus, Antigone)

Sophocles Plays: Two
(Ajax, Women of Trachis, Electra, Philoctetes)

Methuen Student Editions

John Arden	*Serjeant Musgrave's Dance*
Alan Ayckbourn	*Confusions*
Aphra Behn	*The Rover*
Edward Bond	*Lear*
Bertolt Brecht	*The Caucasian Chalk Circle*
	Life of Galileo
	Mother Courage and her Children
Anton Chekhov	*The Cherry Orchard*
Caryl Churchill	*Top Girls*
Shelagh Delaney	*A Taste of Honey*
John Galsworthy	*Strife*
Robert Holman	*Across Oka*
Henrik Ibsen	*A Doll's House*
Charlotte Keatley	*My Mother Said I Never Should*
Bernard Kops	*Dreams of Anne Frank*
Federico García Lorca	*Blood Wedding*
	The House of Bernarda Alba
	(bilingual edition)
John Marston	*The Malcontent*
Willy Russell	*Blood Brothers*
Wole Soyinka	*Death and the King's Horseman*
August Strindberg	*The Father*
J. M. Synge	*The Playboy of the Western World*
Oscar Wilde	*The Importance of Being Earnest*
Tennessee Williams	*A Streetcar Named Desire*
Timberlake Wertenbaker	*Our Country's Good*

For a Complete Catalogue of Methuen Drama titles
write to:

Methuen Drama
215 Vauxhall Bridge Road
London SW1V 1EJ